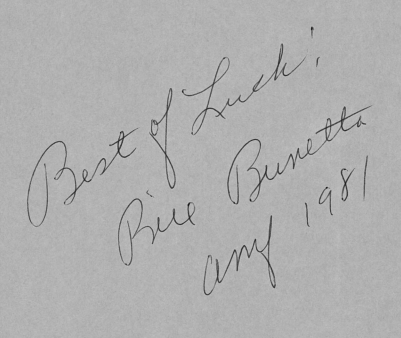

Best of Luck!
Bill Bunetta
amf 1981

The perfect Game

The perfect Game

the world of bowling

by Herman Weiskopf

A Rutledge Book
Published by Prentice-Hall, Inc.
Englewood Cliffs, N.J.

Editorial
Fred R. Sammis
John Sammis
Jeremy Friedlander
Beverlee Galli
Jay Hyams
Art Direction
Allan Mogel
Production
Lori Stein

Prepared and produced by Rutledge Books, Inc.,
25 West 43rd Street, New York, N.Y. 10036.
Published in 1978 by Prentice-Hall, Inc.,
Englewood Cliffs, New Jersey.
Copyright 1978 by Rutledge Books in all countries
of the International Copyright Union. All rights reserved.
Printed in Germany.

Library of Congress Cataloging in Publication Data
Weiskopf, Herman.
   The perfect game.
   "A Rutledge book."
   Includes Index.
   1. Bowling. 2. Bowling—History. I. Title.
GV903.W42   796.6   77-19111
ISBN: 0-13-657015-1

Consulting Editor
Bill Bunetta
Contributing Editors
Jim Dressel (chapter 4)
Remo Picchietti (chapter 5)
Special photography
Photography taken especially for
The Perfect Game by:
Jack and Peter Mecca (chapter 3)
Peter Read Miller (chapter 3—color—and chapter 6)
Al Panzera (chapter 4)
Ken Sherfinski (chapter 1 and 2)
Color shading of photographs in chapter 7 by Allan Weitz

Contents

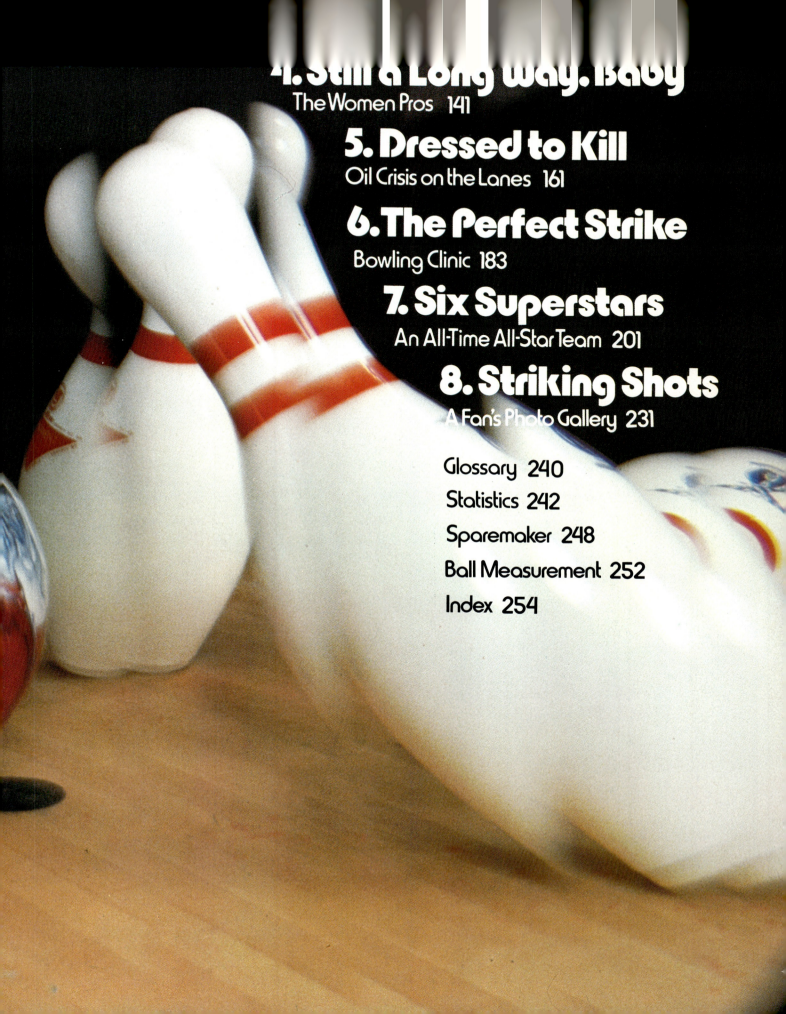

PLR 1											TOT	HDP
1 M	72	9/	7/	X	7/	63	72				100	100
2 K	43	63	7-	6/	7/	63	8/				65	65
3 J	72	8/	7/	72	9/	62	8/				76	76
4 T	9/	7/	X	72	8/	7/					82	82
5												
6												

TONY   G 1 F 7   353   353

A Game for Everyone
Bowling Today

When a 1971 survey by the Louis Harris pollsters revealed that more Americans took part in bowling than in any other year-round sport —51.8 million—it seemed the game had reached its zenith. Four years later (1975) the Harris organization looked again at sports participation in America. This time it found that the number of Americans who bowled at least once a year had risen a whopping 25.3 percent to 64.9 million. A survey by Target Group Index in the spring of 1977 estimated the tenpin population to be 63.7 million.

Who are all these bowlers and where are they coming from? The answer appears to be just about everybody, and from just about everywhere. Bowling has sold itself across the broad spectrum of American society—to women as well as men; to different ethnic, social, age, cultural, and income groups; across geographic boundaries; and all despite economic tribulations within the industry and in the country at large. Bowling is, quite simply, *the* American participant sport—the real national pastime, if you will.

Some statistics: Both the Harris and Target Group Index studies showed that the bowling population is better educated than the nation as a whole. About 40 percent of bowlers have a college background, about 5 percent more than the general population. In addition adult bowlers show a median income of $16,290, 17.4 percent above the national average. As the Harris survey put it, "Bowling was found to increase in popularity as income and educational levels rise." Finally, the bowling population is considerably younger than the national average age. Some 40 percent of America's bowlers are between the ages of 18 and 34, compared to 28 percent of the total population. These and many other figures are cited to indicate that bowling is likely to remain massively popular, as Americans as a whole grow older, better educated, and more prosperous.

Bowling is often perceived as a sport of the 1950s, for it was at that time that it burst upon American life as a recreational craze. Yet the game has a very contemporary appeal, as well as a tradiional one. In assembly-lined, Madison-Avenued, skyrised, credit-carded, political-scandalized, energy-crunched, computerized America, recreational sports have become a more welcome outlet than ever, and bowling has more than held its own against the trendier sports of tennis, golf, skiing, and jogging. In an era when men and women are looking increasingly for sports they can participate in together, mixed bowling leagues, once almost unknown, have grown to 63 percent of the total. Americans struggling to keep up with inflation find the price is right for both a bowling game and the equipment it requires of the bowler. While other recreational facilities suffer from long waiting times and overcrowding, bowling lanes continue to be eminently accessible. And the game itself, easy to learn though difficult to master, makes an ideal activity for a sports-minded person without the time for extensive lessons.

Then, too, bowling lately has attracted people with its new, highly attractive centers. A mini-building boom in the mid- and late seventies has produced centers with lavish accoutrements: chandeliers, palm trees, fountains, colorful decors, gourmet restaurants, and waitresses dressed to enhance the lanes' motif, from western to colonial to outer space. At some bowling centers waitresses scoot around the concourse behind the lanes in motorized carts, serving drinks and snacks. In others carpeting has been installed on the walls, reducing noise from the lanes. Still others offer dancing to live bands in their night clubs.

These, among other features, attract people to bowling and, in some measure, keep them returning to the game. But to prosper bowling needs more than a casually committed constituency. Approximately 70 percent of all bowling is league bowling, the crux of the proprietor's business, and of the entire industry. To persuade bowlers to make a weekly date at the lanes, no small commitment in the less structured life styles of the seventies, bowling relies heavily on its grassroots organizations: the all-male American Bowling Congress (ABC) and its 4.5 million members in 1977, the Women's International Bowling Congress (WIBC), 4 million members, and the American Junior Bowling Congress (AJBC), 800,000 members. This "Big Three" comprises not only the largest but one of the best-run governing bodies of any sport in America.

The ABC, preeminent member of the three, checks all lanes and sanctions only those that meet its specifications. Few proprietors disdain such sanction, for the Big Three only issues awards for bowling done at such certified establishments. The ABC also formulates standards for equipment, which the industry is careful to heed. In 1977, the ABC opened an elaborate testing facility in Greendale, Wisconsin (close to Milwaukee), behind the already impressive building that houses the headquarters of all three organizations. There the ABC's

staff of technicians carries on extensive tests to find solutions to problems of lanes maintenance, ball hardness, and pin weight, among others, which have become important issues in the industry. (See Chapter 5.)

The ABC, WIBC, and AJBC all charge their members a minimal amount for dues, in return for which they provide many similar services: bonding and insurance to safeguard league and association funds; supplies such as rulebooks, schedules, and record-keeping forms for leagues; state and local championships run through the parent body's local affiliates; national championships; and a court of appeals to settle disputes. Extensive awards programs dispense trophies, plaques, chevrons, and other keepsakes for high scores, improved scoring, championship teams and their sponsors, difficult spare conversions, and other items. Together the Big Three distribute more than two million awards each year, a feat worthy of an award itself.

The six ABC field representatives and WIBC's five serve as a liaison between the central organizations and the bowlers. These field representatives conduct meetings with proprietors and bowlers, answer technical questions, settle minor disputes, and in general do what they can to keep the game and the organization running smoothly in their regions. In a tradition established early in the life of the ABC, state and local chapters function autonomously within the guidelines of the governing body. Some even conduct their own lane inspections.

Although the ABC and WIBC share the same headquarters, they operate separately, each with its own departments for mailing (tons of material annually), public relations, certifications, rules, memberships, bonding, awards, and field services. Each organization holds a yearly convention and tournament. At their tournament the men compete in a regular division for five-man teams with averages of 850 or less; a booster division for teams averaging more than 850; a classic division, essentially for professionals; a double-elimination masters category for high-average men (giving local bowlers a chance to roll against the game's biggest names); and a senior division for older bowlers. The women have three divisions: an open division for the best bowlers and first and second divisions for lesser bowlers. Each division has singles, doubles, all-events, and teams championships, and there is a Queens tournament that corresponds to the ABC Masters.

In addition to running their own tournaments and assisting in those of their affiliates, the ABC and WIBC sanction independent tournaments, such as the Hoinke Classic in Cincinnati, which attracts fifty thousand bowlers each year. Why? Mostly because it offers $1 million in prizes, including $25,000 to the victorious doubles pair, $34,000 to the high-scoring team, and $46,000 to the top singles shooter. According to bowling rules, a bowler remains an amateur no matter how much money he earns on the lanes unless he joins one of the play-for-pay associations.

Bowling counts a hard-core constituency of more than nine million people, in ABC, WIBC, and AJBC membership. Each year each group holds a mammoth national tournament. Left: the opening of the 1977 ABC tournament, in Reno, Nevada.

Chicago's Petersen Classic, a nine-month-long event still held at Archer-35th Recreation in Chicago, where it began in 1921, ranks as the most distinctive of the independent tournaments. It is not sanctioned by the ABC or WIBC, and Tournament Director Mark Collor prefers it just that way. The Petersen guarantees its bowlers inconsistent lane conditions and, should anyone begin to score heavily, a marvelous variety of other problems: mechanical breakdowns, dropped pins, a cat meandering through the lanes, a pigeon hovering above them, blasts of frigid air, blaring announcements, alleys sunken beneath pools of oil. It's all part of the Petersen policy of calculated neglect. Collor explains, "Years ago I took it all seriously when people complained about our conditions. Then I learned that bowlers enjoy all this stuff. So we play it up. Our lane conditions are maintained conscientiously: the same for everybody—miserable. But equal. To keep scores down. We want to give duffers a chance to win. That's what the Petersen is all about. If we didn't keep scores low, the little guys wouldn't have a chance."

Each year thirty thousand bowlers come to the Petersen, lured by the $800,000 prize fund and the promise of misadventures even an ABC lane inspector would have to smile at.

One other note about the grassroots of bowling. Many handicapped men and women unable to take part in any other sport—among them stroke victims, amputees, the blind, even quadriplegics—have become bowlers. Blind bowlers use a guide rail; more severely handicapped bowlers use a ball drop, a device of aluminum tubing with a notch at the uppermost level to cradle the ball and a small wheel at the bottom to send it on line toward the pins. Once the bowler feels his shot has been lined up, he pulls a release string that sends the ball down the ball drop and on its way to the pins. The American Blind Bowling Association, the American Wheelchair Bowling Association, and the National Deaf Bowling Association all hold annual national championships.

In addition to the different organizations representing the recreational bowler, the bowling community consists of three other elements: the manufacturers, of which AMF and Brunswick are the largest members; the proprietors, represented by the Bowling Proprietors' Association of America (BPAA); and the pro bowlers, both men and

As of 1977, there were approximately 24 million bowlers under the age of 18, or 37% of the total bowling population. Combined with the 25 million bowlers (40%) between 18 and 34, young bowlers give the sport a far more youthful constituency than most people think it has.

Opposite: *Offering exercise without demanding strenuous exertion, bowling has a special appeal to the elderly.*
Right: *The game's rhythm and coordination are not lost on the handicapped.*
Below: *Wheelchair bowlers are extraordinary, impressive athletes.*

women. These groups have formed an umbrella organization, the National Bowling Council (NBC), to centralize the marketing of bowling. The NBC has pioneered in standardizing bowling teaching methods and, through its clinics, instructors' training. The NBC also conducts major promotional campaigns and runs the National Collegiate Bowling Championship.

On one front, however, the NBC and its member organizations have been almost stymied. Bowling still suffers acutely from a bad reputation among many of the country's opinion makers, as it has more often than not since its earliest days in America. (See Chapter 2.) William ("Bucky") Woy described this attitude well when he was commissioner of the Professional Women Bowlers' Association (PWBA), trying to drum up sponsors for the women's tour. Woy said, "One of the problems is the image of bowling. I don't care what a lot of officials or bowling 'leaders' say to the contrary, bowling still has a long way to go, image-wise, with the people who count—the people you have to convince to shell out for those $100,000 prize funds. They still think the average bowler is a steamfitter, a carpenter, or a garbageman. Don't tell me different. I talk to these guys in their walnut- or mahogany-paneled suites. You think they bowl every weekend or every Wednesday afternoon? Well, they don't. They play golf or tennis or go sailing. They still think the average bowling center is two floors down in the basement under some bar or pool room."

As Woy noted, the people who deride bowling do so largely out of ignorance. Never having bowled seriously, they fail to appreciate the skills the game demands. They probably caught glimpses of it on television shows such as "Laverne and Shirley" or "Candid Camera," which have tended to present the game as one for buffoons and clods. These myths have proved difficult to dispel. (See Chapter 3, on the public relations problems of pro bowlers.)

Bowling is decidedly not chic. It has never had the upper crust tradition of golf, sailing, skiing, or tennis. It can't claim the dynamism of violence that lends glamour to sports such as boxing, football, and ice hockey. And it isn't a sport to make you physically fit, such as basketball, soccer, or jogging. It is, for better and worse, a game of skill, coordination, and, perhaps most of all, concentration, as challenging and complex as you make it. To the uninitiated that is just not glamorous enough. But as most sportspeople know, glamour doesn't make a sport satisfying. Bowling is a people sport—

ideal both for good fellowship and stimulating competition, in addition to the individual challenges it presents. Time and again, people who know bowling cite this human element as its most appealing characteristic.

Perhaps it is best described by a man whose business is to visit bowling centers. John Jowdy has been a combination distributor-dealer-salesman-public relations man for Columbia Industries, Inc. since 1962, and in his travels he has come to appreciate the almost old-fashioned friendliness he finds at certain centers.

"Most of my stops are at the pro shops in bowling centers," Jowdy says. "Some of these places have a marvelous atmosphere that makes you want to just sit and talk and gossip and listen for hours. That's just what a lot of people do in these pro shops. My favorite is Pinky's Pro Shop in Harper Woods, Michigan, a suburb of Detroit. Pinky Marchione was the proprietor until recently. His place has the atmosphere I had in mind. There is a bulletin board where people tack up the latest news about marriages, deaths, and things that happened to local folks. It's not unusual at a place like Pinky's for a card to be placed on the bulletin board for all bowlers to sign to wish somebody a happy marriage or to wish them a speedy recovery. Donations are sometimes taken for those who are sick or to send flowers.

"Back near the end of the room is a coffee urn and a box of rolls or doughnuts. There's also a plate there, sort of an honor system so people can deposit a dime or quarter or whatever they feel is right for the amount of stuff they drink or eat. . . . Starting at about 9:30 in the morning and then for the rest of the day, there are always at least four or five guys in the room. Sometimes there are twenty. They discuss bowling and other sports. There are plenty of friendly arguments about the great bowlers of the past and present. These people also sit and talk about the weather and other things and get to know each other in a delightful way. They come on the way to work, on the way home from work. What they come for is the flavor of the place and to enjoy each other's company. I've got a lot of other places like this that I enjoy visiting."

Beneath its shiny veneer of new and glamorous centers, recreational bowling is more unassuming and congenial than it is imposing. Some people who don't know the game usually miss this simple friendliness. Some bowling people appear embarrassed by it, as if it somehow isn't enough. But those like John Jowdy, who understand the game's special character, wouldn't have it any other way.

Celebrity bowlers have both celebrated the game and spoofed it, presenting bowling as a cultural stereotype or silly diversion as well as a serious sport. Above: Bob Newhart; opposite left: *Penny Marshall (right) and Cindy Williams as LaVerne and Shirley;* opposite right: *Sid Caesar.*

17

I. A Pastime's Forgotten Past

Early History

For want of a better name, the case at hand may be called "the Sinister Disappearance of Tenpins' Past." It's one of those perplexing mysteries of murder without a body left behind—there's plenty of mystery, but where's the crime?

The facts, Inspector:

We all know the fellow we're looking for—T. P. Bowling, an eccentric old sport: born in Egypt; disappeared for five or six thousand years; surfaced in Germany (Herr Kegel), where he got religion and prospered; turned seedy in England, where the gamblers and other low-life types got to him; and washed up in America with some other Old World sludge. Most of us don't recall hearing of him again until the 1890s or so, when the newly energized and soon-to-be-organized proprietors of the game picked up the old fellow, dusted him off, and made him into something of a gay blade. Since then, he's developed into a real superstar, one of those country rubes worth a bundle.

Recognize the guy? Sure. So where's the mystery, and did you say murder? Well, if you'll just take off those aviator rose-colored glasses for a moment, Inspector, you'll realize that that wasn't much of a dossier on a seven-thousand-year-old man. We really know very little about the origins and developments of this sport. That neat-looking bowling crowd has been up to a mean trick; while everyone else has been discovering their roots, bowlers have pretty much buried theirs. An unfriendly DA might call that nothing less than killing off the past, and if that isn't murder, well, it's at least an unwholesome cover-up, certainly no way to treat a distinguished senior citizen.

Wait a minute, you object. What about all the bowling on the green in colonial times, and lawn bowling, and Francis Drake breaking off a game to vanquish the Spanish Armada, and Henry VIII bowling with his fellow swells? Surely in these commonly known customs and stories there is plenty of bowling lore that has been faithfully preserved. Sorry, sport, that is a different game entirely. It is bowling at a jack (a small marker of some kind), rather than at pins, and with the purpose not of knocking over the target but of placing the ball as close to it as possible. You might as well try to palm off boccie as baseball. (It's just not cricket.)

Give yourself a gutter ball in the first frame.

So with your permission, Inspector, let's re-

Bowling seems to have begun independently in many places, yet the German game (below) was probably the most influential. Overleaf: This bowling, among the London aristocracy in the seventeenth century, probably came from the Dutch, who in turn got a similar game from the Germans.

Top: *Bowling implements discovered by Sir Flinders Petrie at an Egyptian gravesite and dated about 5200 B.C.* Middle and bottom: *Fourteenth century engravings of a form of bowling played with a stick instead of a ball–kayles. These were found by Joseph Strutt and included in his famous book,* The Sports and Pastimes of the People of England *(1801). Opposite: The narrow alley, a staple of the early German game, shown here in a Dutch version about two hundred years old.*

open this matter. I think you'll find it rather exciting really. Bowling's past has been suffocating under a pile of false notions we've been too quick to call history. If we hurry, we might be in time to breathe some life into the old boy, yet.

It would be nice to be able to report that the first strike in bowling history was rolled by Abdul Gizeh at the Sphinx Alleys in Cairo in 7202 B.C., and that Hans Heinrich of Muggendorf, Germany, faced the first 5-7 split on the Continent in A.D. 466. Of course, it won't be that easy. We just don't know who the Abduls and Hanses and other pioneers of bowling were. There has been speculation that prehistoric man indulged in some form of bowling, but archeologists have yet to unearth the computer printout scoresheets for the Neanderthal Nightly Nomad League.

One archeologist, though, did come up with most significant findings concerning the antiquity of bowling at pins. Sir Flinders Petrie, emeritus professor of Egyptology at the University of London, revealed in *The Making of Egypt*, published in 1939, that he had found a complete set of bowling implements at a large gravesite where a child had been buried about 5200 B.C., in the late Gerzean Age. There were several small stone balls, three pieces of marble, and nine slender pins. Petrie surmised that the Egyptians played a game in which they rolled the balls through a small wicketlike gateway, formed by the marble pieces. Their target, he wrote, was the nine pins, arranged in a diamond formation. Thus a forerunner to tenpins may well have been played more than seven thousand years ago.

There is a gap of many centuries before the next trace of bowling at pins surfaces. William Pehle, a German historian and bowler, wrote in his book *Bowling* that the game began in his country during the third century, not as a sport but rather a religious rite. Germans of the time carried a club-like weapon called a *Kegel*. According to Pehle, they would place the *Kegel* at one end of a church cloister and roll a ball at it from the other end. The *Kegel* symbolized the *Heide*, or heathen, and if these first "keglers" (as bowlers are still called today) succeeded in toppling the *Kegel*, they had symbolically slain the heathen. Obviously, those who did

The Germans exported both their game and its Gemutlichkeit *to their neighbors in Switzerland (opposite)* and Poland *(right).* But there was apparently nothing quite like the rustic flavor of the original version. Above: *a painting entitled* After the Match.

24

showed themselves to be living exemplary Christian lives. At the end of the session, they were praised and toasted at banquets. Those who missed were invited to try again another day, and were advised in the meantime to attend to their spiritual lives, which, as the still-standing *Kegel*/heathen suggested, wanted improvement. Many Germans took part in these rituals, which apparently started as nothing more than object lessons but grew to hold great religious significance.

How the religious significance diminished and the recreational atmosphere grew we don't know. Evidently the Church itself helped in the transformation. In the cities of Hildersheim and Halberstam, the clergy competed at the game with the town's divinity students—the first bowling league, of sorts. Bowling became a regular event at village dances, country festivals, and even baptisms. Among the many references to the game that Pehle found in Germany of the Middle Ages and later was one at a huge venison feast in Frankfurt in 1463. He also discovered that in 1518 the city of Breslau bestowed a valuable prize on the winner of a bowling event there: an ox.

Martin Luther (1483-1546), who made a name for himself objecting to the excesses of the Church, found bowling not only irreproachable but elevating. According to Dr. A. L. Graebener's biography of Luther, the clergyman built an alley for his children, bowled with them occasionally, and "enjoyed their laughter when the ball went astray but reminded those who laughed that in ordinary life many a person thinks that he can excel others and will strike down all nine pins . . . and then misses all of them." Thus did the great religious reformer combat the sin of pride.

How the number of pins came to be nine is another mystery. Around 1300, bowlers in some sections of Germany were rolling at three pins, in other sections as many as seventeen. Most early alleys were beds of clay, slate, or cinders, but by 1200, bowlers in Germany and the adjacent countries of Holland and Switzerland, to which the game had spread, were rolling on a single wooden plank, sometimes only a foot or so wide. The pins were placed on a somewhat wider platform (36 to 48 inches wide) at the end of the plank. Alleys of this sort were still very much in evidence in twentieth-century Germany.

The Germans were not the only Europeans who bowled at pins. The French, English, and Spanish did too. In his definitive work *The Sports and Pastimes of the People of England* (1801), Joseph Strutt traced a primitive English form of bowling at pins, called "kayles," to the French game *quilles*, which means pins, and concluded these games were the forerunners of the English form of ninepins.

Describing two drawings of kayles he found in fourteenth-century manuscripts, Strutt wrote, "In the one instance there are six pins and in the other eight.... One of them in both cases is taller than the rest, and this, I presume, was the king-pin.... The arrangement of the kayle-pins differs greatly from that of the ninepins, the latter being placed upon a square frame in three rows, and the former in one row only. [In] ... club-kayles ... a club or cudgel was thrown at [the pins]."

One is tempted to speculate—was the club that Strutt mentions in his description of kayles some offshoot of the German *Kegel*, which was itself a club when not used as a target? Perhaps, and yet like other forms of kayles, Strutt attributes club-kayles only to a French game, *yeux de quilles à baston*. No doubt the Germans were not the only people in the Middle Ages to carry truncheons and to wind up using them for sport as well as battle.

The English version of the *Kegel* may have been a sheep's bone. An Elizabethan play called *The Longer Thou Livest the More Fool Thou Art* had a dunce who boasted of his skill "At skales, and playing with sheepes-joynte." "Skales" was a form of kayles, and the "sheepes-joynte" was a bowling pin in a version of bowling called "loggats," which Shakespeare's Hamlet referred to when he wondered, "Did these bones cost no more the breeding, but to play at loggats with them?" Strutt quoted one Thomas Hammer as observing that the players of loggats threw at the pins "with another bone instead of bowling."

Apparently, toppling over pins, whether clubs or bones, with a ball or another club or bone, was not an idea unique to Germany. If it wasn't a heathen one was symbolically slaying, then it could have been a whole cluster of infidels, with their leader represented by the larger pin in the middle. In 1651, Sir Thomas Urquhart observed that the Roundheads agitating against the policies of Charles II "may be said to use the king as the

*One English offshoot of bowling took its name from its motivation—
to "bubble the justice," that is, to evade the restrictions on
bowling by concocting a game that wasn't really bowling. Nine holes
replaced the nine pins, and bowling became a bit like miniature golf.*

27

The English game of skittles could be very much like German bowling (complete with hobbled pinboys, right), or closer to the English game of bowls, with its biased ball. In the illustration above, a lithograph copy of the painting Skittle Players Outside an Inn, by Jan Steeh, the game seems to be half-bowls, a cross between bowls and bowling at pins.

players at nine-pins do the middle kayle, which they call the king, at whose fall they aim, the sooner to the gaining of their prize.'' Perhaps it was through some symbolic rendition of battle that bowling at pins got its start.

As kayles was developing into ninepins in England, *quilles* was becoming a distinctive ninepin game in France. The game featured thin pins more than a yard tall, each with a knob 6¾ inches in circumference at the top and a similarly bulbous belly. The nine pins stood precariously balanced on square blocks of wood in a playing court 22 feet square, with an 8-foot gap between pins. Thus, there was a pin at every corner, at the midpoint of every side, and in the middle of the square. The ball was 31 inches in circumference and weighed 10 pounds 6 ounces. It was carved from walnut and had a hand-carved grip, consisting of two slots, one five inches wide, the other half that width—evidently for the fingers and thumb. Both the pins and the ball resembled those unearthed in California in the 1930s and identified as remnants of the Basque settlers from Spain. Perhaps the Spanish and French games were related.

The bowler in *quilles* stood near one of the corner pins and struck it by swinging the ball at it. If he did it properly, he knocked the pin into one of its neighbors, which in turn took out a third pin. Thus a whole row of pins could be felled. Then the bowler released the ball, trying to topple the center pin and cause it to roll or spin on its belly, knocking over the other pins. If the bowler managed to keep his ball inside the court, he won another shot, taken from the spot where the ball came to rest.

This procedure faintly resembled the English game of skittles, which combined elements of loggats and ninepins as well. ('' 'I'll cleave you from the skull to the twist and make nine skittles of thy bones,' '' Strutt quotes a character from the play *The Merry Milk-maid of Islington*—1680.) In skittles, the player bowled his first ball at the cluster of ninepins, and if he did not topple them all, he moved much closer for his second ball, which he dropped or ''tipped'' among them, evidently with as much spin as possible.

In some forms of the game the skittle ball was circular but not spherical, having flat sides. This suggests the old and honorable English game of bowls, in which the balls are flattened on one side in order to move along a curved path to the jack.

Most American histories of pin bowling have blithely adopted the history of bowling at a jack as if it were just another stage in the evolution of bowling at pins. It wasn't; it was a different game— as different as ''lawn bowling,'' as Americans call bowls, is from bowling today. But the two forms were related. For example, the bias of the skittle ball and that of the bowl may well have had a common ancestor. In *Touchers and Rubs on Ye Ancient Royale Game of Bowles* (1893) (a little book as intriguing as its title), Humphrey J. Dingley speculated that the skittle ball and all biased balls originated with the discus of the ancients, who may have found sport not only in hurling but in tossing or even rolling it. This would also make the game of quoits, in which one tosses rings (disks with a hole in them), an ancient cousin of bowling (both varieties). The backhand flip one uses to toss the biased skittle ball bears a telling resemblance to the motion with which one tosses a quoit. This kind of release can be found even in modern ten-pin bowling, among such bowlers as the well-known pro, Paul Colwell.

Pin bowling and bowls probably combined to breed the rather intricate game of half-bowls, described by a commentator in the fifteenth century. In this game, 15 conical pins were stood in a flattened, elongated circle, with one in the middle (the king-pin) and two extending from the far side. The bowler threw a half-ball (not really a biased bowl, just a half-sphere) so that it rolled around the circle, including the two backside pins, and first contacted the pins as it was actually curving back toward the bowler.

Kayles, cloish (kayles with a ball), loggats, half-bowl were all English games that seemed to develop independently of the German forms of bowling at pins. Skittles showed what might have been a Germanic influence in the use of nine pins and in the variety called ''Dutch skittles'' or ''Dutch pins,'' in which the pins, particularly the center, king-pin, were taller and thinner than the chunky skittle pins. (There was no king-pin in skittles.) But the English game that showed the greatest similarity to German pin bowling was what Strutt called ''long-bowling,'' which he discovered in London in the eighteenth century. He wrote, ''It was performed in a narrow enclosure, about twenty or thirty yards in length, and at the farther end was placed a square frame with nine small pins upon it;

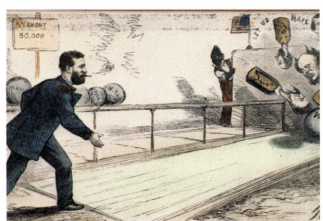

Left: *Wedge-shaped pins replaced the conical ones in England by the nineteenth century, but the old practice of "tippling"—shooting from close to the target—continued.*
Top: *The leisurely rural German pastime remained very much the same into the twentieth century.* Above: *By the 1870s, bowling had become common enough in America that a supporter of Ulysses S. Grant put him in the guise of a bowler to score political points.*

at these pins the players bowled in succession; and a boy, who stood by the frame to set up the pins that were beat down by the bowl, called out the numbers, which [were] placed to the account of the player; and the bowl was returned by the means of a small trough, placed with a gradual descent from the pins to the bowlers, on one side of the enclosure. Some call this game Dutch-rubbers."

For all the forms in which they bowled at pins, the English probably added little to the substance of the game as it would take hold in America. But they did make an important stylistic contribution. The game that was wholesome, jolly fun in Germany, the English managed to make thoroughly disreputable.

Blame it partly on aristocratic pretensions. Bowls was the game for the upper classes, notwithstanding the difficulty several English kings encountered in trying to limit it to the aristocracy. Bowling at pins was left mostly to the common people. In *Sport and Society: Elizabeth to Anne* (1969), Dennis Brailsford quoted Sir Thomas Elyot (1490-1546) on "pynnes and Keyting" (i.e., skittles and quoits): "[to be] utterly objected of all noble men."

Excluded from the realm of gracious amateurs, bowling at pins quickly became the province of seedy professionals—the hustlers and gamblers—as well as those commonfolk whose sporting lives were slightly more scrupulous. The first public bowling alleys opened in London in the fifteenth century, and though the term "alley" as used at about this time usually referred to an indoor or sheltered court for bowls, it is likely that sooner or later all sorts of diversions, including bowling at pins, were pursued in establishments like these, strategically located near hotels and taverns, where they could attract their roguish clientele. Strutt wrote that the alleys "were productive of very evil consequences, for they became not only exceedingly numerous, but were often attached to places of public resort, which rendered them the receptacles of idle and dissolute persons. . . . In the fifteenth and sixteenth centuries these nurseries of vice were universally decried. . . ."

So both bowls and bowling at pins suffered. Various attempts to ban the games succeeded most notably in encouraging new, equally unelevating forms. Strutt recalled one eighteenth-century magistrate who "caused all the skittle-frames in or about the city of London to be taken up, and prohibited the playing of dutch pins, ninepins, or in long bowling allies, [whereupon] in many places the game of nine-holes was revived as a substitute, with the new name of Bubble the Justice, because the populace had taken it into their heads to imagine, that the power of the magistrates extended only to the prevention of such pastimes as were specified by name in the public acts, and not to any new species of diversion."

In the game of nine-holes, the ninepins were simply replaced with holes into which the player tried to toss or roll a ball. A verse from the chil-

dren's book *Poor Robin* (1707) probably referred to some version of it:

> People to Moorfields flock in sholes.
>
> At nine pins and at pigeon holes.

In eighteenth-century London, bowling at pins became even more firmly a game for the poor and disreputable when a building boom left the commoner with only bowling centers or the streets for playing fields. Strutt noted that the "general decay of manly and spirited exercise" such as archery could be traced to the "want of places proper for the purpose . . . so that if it were not for skittles, dutch-pins, four corners [a form of skittles], and the like pastimes, [the people] would have no amusements for the exercise of the body; and these amusements are only to be met with in places belonging to common drinking houses."

So much for the English. The game as they brought it to America was similarly entrenched in the tavern, as were a good many other diversions of colonial life. If it had been left to the English colonists, it probably would have stayed there, harassed as it was in England. In *Four Centuries of Sport in America (1490-1890)*, Herbert Manchester reports, "In 1647 in Massachusetts Bay . . . we have a court order against shuffleboard. . . . In 1650 this prohibition was extended against 'bowling or any other play of game in or about howses of common entertaynment.'"

Among the Dutch in New York, the game was among a list of activities banned on Sundays: "Dancing, Card-playing, Tick-tacking [a form of backgammon], Playing at ball, at bowls, at ninepins; taking jaunts in Boats, Wagons or Carriages."

However, other Dutch settlers were evidently kinder to the game. The reference in Washington Irving's *Sketch Book* (1819) to the legendary Rip Van Winkle being awakened from his lengthy

The French played a game called quatre coins, *or "four corners,"* above, *as well as a more traditional form of bowling later,* opposite. *The later game may have come from the distinctively French form called* quilles, *which featured huge pins and balls with hand-carved grips.*

slumber by the sound of little men bowling at pins indicates that the game was well known among the Dutch in New York's Hudson River Valley.

Still, it was left to the Germans to develop the game in the New World. The first German settlers arrived in 1683, and by the time of the Revolution Germans comprised the third largest white ethnic group in the colonies. However, it was not until the massive German migrations of the mid-nineteenth century that the game began to boom.

The reminiscences of one Andrew Rohn, recorded in the 1904 edition of the *Bowling Encyclopedia,* edited by John G. Hemmer and W. J. Kenna, are a peak at the game and the surroundings in which it was played by these immigrants. Rohn, a bowling proprietor in Chicago at the turn of the century, remembered the early days of bowling in the area (a major German-American center):

"Fifty years ago the only bowlers were Germans and the only alleys were the very crude ones at the picnic groves and other German resorts. When we wanted to bowl we made up a party of our friends, ladies and gentlemen, hired a wagon and drove ten, fifteen or twenty miles to one of our favorite picnic gardens. We started early in the morning, carried a goodly supply of eatables and went prepared to spend the entire day, returning as a rule considerably after dusk. . . .

"Alleys were in the open air, exposed to all changes of the weather. The boards soon became warped, and of course, no attempt was ever made to polish the alleys or even to keep them in fair condition. It was rough and ready bowling, where everyone tried to have a pleasant time socially, with little or no thought as to who was the champion roller."

This was the spirit that the game as played among German-Americans would retain until at least the turn of the century. As it no doubt was in Germany, bowling among German-Americans was really part of a folk festival. But one of the games Rohn described was very different from the modern version. The scoring went from 200 down, so the winner was the one who reached zero first. Each player bowled three balls per frame, even if he achieved a strike or a spare; the pins were simply respotted for a second or third ball if necessary. Most interesting of all, a bowler scored more points (36) for leaving the five-pin, or king-pin, and toppling the rest than for a strike (30).

This form of the game must have been quite similar to the German version. John Andresen, in 1977 the president of the Williamsburg Bowling Club of New York (founded 1877), remembered that as a pinboy in 1908, at an outdoor alley in Germany, he witnessed a remarkably similar game. Whenever a bowler knocked down all the pins but the king-pin, which was taller and heavier than the rest and decorated with a carved wooden cross, he favored the pinboy with a tip.

As the community with the largest German population, New York became the bowling capital of America in the nineteenth century. The first indoor center (Knickerbocker Alleys, with lanes of baked clay) opened on January 1, 1840, in Manhattan. (Chicago gained its first indoor alley only after the Civil War, according to Rohn.) Indoor bowling quickly became a fad in New York. "In 1849, it reached its zenith," reported A. G. Spalding's *Standard Rules for Bowling in the United States* (1887). "On Broadway from Barclay Street to Eighth Street, there were alleys to be found on every block."

Apparently, the sudden popularity of the game did it more harm than good, at least in the short run. The gamblers and hustlers sprang up in America as they had in England, and the game was once again subjected to governmental ban. The story goes that tenpins owed its invention to one of these bans, when someone added a tenth pin to circumvent a prohibition against ninepins. It's a nice story, and neatly within the bowling tradition

Society ladies made bowling a genteel diversion in late-nineteenth century America. The print and poem opposite top *suggest that many a man was bowled over by a lady on the lanes.*

Ten-pins all

When Dolly bowls,
    Her sleeve high up her round white arm she rolls.
(The whitest, sweetest arm it is in town —
No wonder that the helpless pins go down!)

Her ball she swings —
    Oh, happy ball, to whom kind fortune brings
To rest a moment in her wilful hand!
(No matter tho' eftsoon you rudely land!)

She poises, slim;
    And now with shining eyes she views it skim,
And laughs to see the damage that she wreaks,
And gleefully another missile seeks.

Most patient pins!
    We know the program through, its outs and ins,
For we stand, likewise, in a silly crew,
And, easy victims, wait what she may do.

She need but glance;
    Delaying for no farther circumstance
Straightway we fall, and abject lie, and then
Let Master Cupid set us up again.

Edwin L. Sabin

established in England of commoners thwarting the designs of those who would tell them what to do. But it's probably not true. A Connecticut law in 1841 had made it illegal to maintain "any Ninepin lane, whether more or less than ninepins are used in such play," and there is no reason to believe that the New York legislature had any less savvy.

The shift to tenpins, however it came about, dramatically changed the game, of course. But at the time, it seemed academic. Bowling was less threatened from without, by restrictive state legislatures, than from within, by unscrupulous promoters who cheapened the game by using larger pins, more closely clustered. "When ten-strike followed ten-strike . . . ," reported Spalding's *Standard Rules*, "bowling soon grew to be monotonous and gradually spun out of existence."

Well, not quite. It was still a favorite of German-Americans, and a new wave of immigrants after the Civil War popularized it again. Many of the early immigrants had been political refugees from the upheavals in Germany in 1848. Idealistic, nationalistic, and strong believers in physical as well as cultural education, they established gymnastic and cultural centers in their American communities, called *Turnvereine*, after a German society of

Knickerbocker Saloon QUICK STEP

COMPOSED AND RESPECTFULLY DEDICATED
TO THE
Proprietors
OF THE
KNICKERBOCKER SALOON.
BY
ADAM STEWART

the same name to which many of them had belonged.

These *Turnvereine* were not bowling centers, but they were centers of cultural life, and some evidently had bowling lanes. Bowling may have been a part of their big yearly *Turnfest* celebrations. With the renewed influx of German immigrants, not only the *Turnvereine* but other German-American recreational societies boomed. "Although these clubs and societies sought to attract the sons and daughters of earlier arrivals, they enjoyed their major success with more recent newcomers, whose sense of loneliness in a strange land was thus assuaged," wrote Blake McKelvey in *Rochester History* (October 1957), describing the German-American community in urban Rochester, New York, as characteristic of the time. The Rochester *Turnfest* drew Germans from Utica, Syracuse, and even Buffalo.

In *The Maryland Germans* (1948), Dieter Cunz wrote that a typical German-American organization was the Baltimore *Schutzengesellschaft*, or shooting club, "which was founded in the middle of the century but did not achieve its greatest development until after the Civil War. It was a kind of country club for lower classes. It owned a park on Belair Avenue with target ranges, dance floors, bowling alleys, banquet rooms, etc. . . . For the large affairs, there were often no less than 20,000 people in the club's park." Apparently wherever German-Americans gathered to celebrate their cultural heritage, bowling was part of the festivities.

German-American bowling clubs began in New York after the Civil War. Drawing their members from different regions or towns in Germany, they functioned like fraternal organizations, in which bowling was only one of many activities for fostering friendships and fun. There were team parties, pig roasts, dances, and picnics, attended by bowlers, their families, and friends. For example, in 1899 in Whitestone, New York, the Mucker club went on an outing that lasted a full day, the festivities including a parade, speeches, lunch, boat rides, bowling by men and women, dinner, the crowning of a king and queen, and the distribution of prizes, among which were 200 cigars, a box of bacon, an umbrella, and two tons of coal. Topping off the evening was "an elaborate fireworks display . . . myriads of red and green lights, sky rockets, Roman candles, etc. . . . *How Can We Bear to Leave Thee*

New York boasted some of the more stylish establishments, and the music to match. The Knickerbocker Alleys were the first indoor lanes in America.

was played by the band as the ship headed down the East River back to Manhattan."

In 1885, these German clubs banded together as the United Bowling Clubs of New York. The group proclaimed itself "a grand organization, similar to the Turner, Saenger, and Schutzen Societies." In its souvenir journal of 1896, it devoted a full page to the picture of Prince Bismarck, "Our Honorary Member," lest there be any doubt where its roots and sympathies lay. In 1891, the United Bowling Clubs sent a delegation to Hannover, Germany, for a bowling festival, and the group visited with the German emperor.

One of the members of that delegation, and of many similar ones to come, was "Uncle" Joe Thum, a guiding force in the United Bowling Clubs and one of the most successful of the game's early bowling proprietors. Thum got his start in 1880, when the owner of the restaurant where he worked gave up and went back to Germany, leaving the place (at 401 Greenwich Street in Manhattan) to Thum. The new owner quickly turned the restaurant into a success and built two lanes in the basement. The traditional German combination of good food and good sport proved popular, and before long Thum was the town's leading bowling proprietor. In 1891, he opened the Germania Bowling Alleys, at 293 Bowery, and in 1896, the famous White Elephant Alleys at Broadway and 31st Street. Like many other ambitious projects, this grand new bowling establishment wasn't supposed to succeed. When it did, it proudly took the name its detractors had given it in expectation of its demise. The *New York Evening Telegram* crowed in its review of opening night, "The spacious room was jammed to the doors with bowling 'cranks,' who cheered the tourney bowlers and congratulated Uncle Joe on his new alleys. There is not a bowling rendezvous in the City that can compare with the White Elephant. The ... alleys with the surroundings are fitted out so elegantly that there was nothing but praise for them last night."

By this time, bowling was well on its way to changing from a German recreational pastime to a major American sport. But the shift was not accomplished easily. Even among Germans, the game took many different forms, and a succession of "ruling bodies" failed for the most part to standardize and regulate it. First, the National Bowling Association (NBA), founded in 1875 by 27 bowling clubs

in Manhattan, set down some rules, including those regulating ball size, the removal of fallen pins from the alley after the first ball, and the distance between the foul line and the center spot of the headpin (60 feet). The group issued a revised set of rules in 1880 but, like the first set, without widespread effect. One commentator at this time called bowling still a "go as you please" game in the East, and no better in the West, where "any rule went." The American Bowling League (ABL) succeeded the National Bowling Association in 1890, and instituted the "20-ball game" by eliminating the use of a third ball in a frame. Thus, the highest possible score was 200, achieved by 10 consecutive strikes. The ABL also reduced the height of the still oversized pins to 15 inches, the standard height today. Many bowlers objected to the ABL's 20-ball game edict, and disputes over professionalism and betting quickly brought about the organization's demise. The American Amateur Bowling League (AABL) followed in 1891, accepting the 20-ball game and taking a hard line that there should be no prize money at tournaments. The latter idea proved so unpopular that it *and* the organization were scuttled over the objections, led by the United Bowling Clubs in New York.

Not until 1895 did bowling manage to form a body strong yet politic enough to govern the game effectively. It is tempting to quip that it was as easy as ABC. It wasn't. The American Bowling Congress (ABC), which today is a prospering and prosperous governing body, took a good 10 years before it could claim to have the game firmly under control. But that is the start of another story—the story of how bowling became a truly American game.

PLR	1	2	3	4	5	6	7	8	9	10	TOT	HDP
1 M	72	9/	7/	X	7/	63	72				100	100
2 K	43	63	7-	6/	7/	63	8/				65	65
3 J	72	8/	7/	72	9/	62	8/				76	76
4 T	9/	7/	X	72	8/	7/	≪				82	82
5												
6												
TONY							G 1 F 7				353	353

PLR	1	2	3	4	5	6	7	8	9	10	TOT	HDP
1 F	9/	72	81	9/	7/	8-	8/	6/			94	94
2 E	53	8/	9-	7/	9/	X	9/	9/			114	114
3 B	53	7/	6/	8-	9/	9-	X	6>			78	78
4 G	8/	X	8/	7/	X	9-	9/				105	105
5												
6												
BOB						G 1	F 8				431	431

2. An American Success Story

...And Never the Twain Shall Meet

In its November 11, 1899, issue, *The Bowlers Journal*, the unofficial organ of the United Bowling Clubs of New York, proclaimed that "in order to start the Twentieth Century, [we] will donate $100 to a Monster Festival." This was the quaint name given by editor Herman Tietz and publisher Louis Schutte to a tournament "in . . . the coming summer, in which teams from all over the country could participate, same to be held under the auspices of the United Bowling Clubs. This would mean an impetus to bowling all over the country, and would help to strengthen and elevate the game."

There was another, less idealistic motive, too, as the paper readily admitted: to "settle once and for all the vexed question of which city can produce the best bowlers." Eastern and midwestern bowlers were eager to do battle, as they had been for decades. The problem was in getting them to agree on the terms of combat.

No one could doubt that the much-desired national competition would not be satisfactorily conducted until the different regional groups could unite under the banner of an organization that would govern the game (and such competition). Unfortunately, the regional rivalries that gave rise to the grand plans for national competition threatened any organization that could bring such plans to fruition. So it was that when the American Bowling Congress began, in 1895 or 1896, depending on whose account one credits, it faced the same seemingly intractable problem that had doomed its three short-lived predecessors: everyone wanted a national organization, and everyone wanted just as badly to go his own way. By the time of the "Monster Festival," or "First International Tournament," as it was more sedately renamed when Canada sent a team, the ABC was not yet strong enough

to conduct such a tournament on its own, but it was getting there.

The impetus for the founding of the ABC came from Tietz, Schutte, and, most of all, Uncle Joe Thum, who in 1895 convinced the United Bowling Clubs, a New York group of 120 teams, that another organization should be formed to step into the breach left by the defunct national governing associations. Organizational meetings were held on July 29, August 26, and September 9, 1895, and on January 13, 1896. The ABC calls the September 9 session, held in Manhattan's Beethoven Hall, its official beginning. There the delegates adopted by a slight margin the system of a 300 maximum score. Until then, the maximum score had been 200, but Louis Stein persuaded his fellow delegates that the new system made the game more attractive by allowing bowlers more room to improve their scores. At this meeting it was also decided to research whether to have 11½- or 12-inch spaces between pins. At the January 13 meeting it was reported that tests proved the 12-inch gap to be more "scientific" and to require more skill from the bowler in downing the pins. The 12-inch standard was adopted, an important rule that helped discourage excessively high scoring.

It was, of course, far easier to adopt rules than to enforce them or, as was more nearly the case, to persuade the various factions to abide by them. At the August 26 meeting, a delegate noted that those present did not have authority to enforce rules—a view that the delegates evidently shared. Here the ABC appeared to learn from the problems of its predecessors. Instead of attempting to demonstrate strength it didn't have, the organization was content to rule, in however limited a way, by consensus. Progress was painfully slow, but more solid.

In 1899, for example, there was talk that the

Overleaf: *Representative American bowlers from early in the century (1909) and today against a theatrical backdrop of the latest technological advance–MagicScore.* Opposite: *the hall where bowling began to put its house in order, the birthplace of the American Bowling Congress.*

Chicago-based Associated Bowling League would secede from the ABC and represent bowlers in the West, which at that time meant nearly every place outside of greater New York. Instead, the Illinois Bowling Association (IBA) embraced Chicago bowlers and kept them in the ABC fold. In fact the IBA did so well at overseeing the sport in its area that autonomy for such local groups eventually became ABC policy. The ABC took another significant step in 1900, when it began to inspect lanes and to certify only those meeting its specifications.

Easterners dominated most of the bowling at the First International Tournament, held in Schuetzen Park, in Union Hill, New Jersey, still the site of German-American cultural festivals today. *The Bowlers Journal* reported that in the intercity team match, however, "The westerners proved the victors, Frank Brill's score of 246 in the first of a three-game block being mainly responsible for the victory. . . . Chicago 2615, New York 2557, Columbus 2543, Wheeling 2535, Brooklyn 2463, Baltimore 2417, St. Louis 2268, Cleveland 2251, Toronto 2169." This climactic event occasioned "quite a few transfers of 'the long green,'" the paper noted.

The next year, 1901, the ABC held its first championships, in Chicago. With some 435 bowlers participating, Frank Brill won the singles title on a strike in the tenth frame. At last the organization appeared to be rolling, only to be nearly derailed the next year.

In 1902 in Buffalo, at the second ABC, East and West clashed headlong in their attempts to control the organization, and they almost wrecked it. The westerners insisted on proxy voting; the easterners opposed it. After much wrangling, most of the Eastern representatives stalked out, and in their absence five officers from the West were elected. Had it not been for two Chicagoans, William V. Thompson and Adrian ("Cap") Anson, the ABC might have succumbed. Thompson was a fine bowler, Anson an alley owner who had been one of the best first basemen and hitters in baseball history. (Many of the founding fathers of bowling in America had played a similar role in baseball, including A. G. Spalding and John G. Hemmer, both of whom helped found the National League. Germans in particular seemed to have this double affinity for bowling and baseball.) At Thompson's behest, Anson talked with Charles Ebbets, the owner of the Brooklyn Dodger baseball team and a leader of the easterners. Anson

Above: *The ABC retained a heavy German accent in its early years, reflecting the still-strong ethnic origins of the game. The Cedarburg, Wisconsin, team at the ABC's 1912 tournament, in Chicago, brought along this piece of folk art— a banner showing a dog (the team's low bowler, apparently) surrounded by mournful pins. Opposite top: 1901 champs, the Standard Bowling Club. Opposite bottom: The 1908 ABC tournament was a Brunswick spectacular.*

discovered Ebbets conducting a meeting at which the eastern representatives were discussing abandoning the ABC and forming their own governing body. Somehow, Anson talked Ebbets out of it. After five hours as ABC president, the West's Charles Pasdeloup resigned when the convention reconvened that night, and all the other new officers followed his lead. The proxy vote was eliminated, and the East-West breakup was averted again.

By 1906 they were at it again, however. A Detroit newspaper account of that year's ABC gathering read, "Easterners withdrew . . . to run another national tournament . . . Antagonism between Chicago and New York is the chief reason . . . Ebbets said, 'I do not think the East and West will ever come together.'"

Above: *The turnout at the 1909 ABC tournament, in Pittsburgh, made for an impressive group portrait.* Opposite: *John ("the Count") Gengler, one of the earliest and greatest hustlers, started bowling in Germany, where he developed an erect stance, a one-step approach, an icy glare, and a disdain for fingerholes.*

Some Stars Are Born

The barons of the game had accepted the idea that bowling should be a national game, with national standards and national champions. They had formed the ABC to promote this vision. However, a few bowlers who functioned largely outside the realm of the ABC probably did more than the organization to liberate the game from its nineteenth-century provinciality. These were the great bowlers of the day, whose reputations reached across the country.

None was more fascinating than John ("the Count") Gengler, a German who came to America about 1905. He was tall and ramrod straight of posture. He dressed impeccably, in a double-breasted suit and top hat, and carried a cane. He was, simply, the greatest hustler in bowling history. Usually, he started off a bowling session with low scores and then, when the ante was raised, displayed his best form. Only someone of great strength and muscular control could have mastered his unique, one-step delivery, which minimized chances for error.

One of Gengler's most extraordinary feats came in Chicago Heights, at lanes he ran for a while. Gengler boasted that he knew those lanes so well that he could bowl on them in the dark, and once he did. His account:

I shot one ball to find the range. Then I had the boys hand me my ball and turn out the lights. When the ball crashed into the pins, the lights were turned on. Sure enough, I had gotten a strike. Because of my delivery, I never had to move from my spot on the approach. I kept rolling strikes in the dark, twelve in a row for a perfect game.

In contrast to the baronial, machinelike Gengler, Jimmy Smith, a Brooklyn boy, wore fashionable wide-striped silk shirts, used a lofty backswing, and took all his shots from the right corner. By 1905, the smooth and stylish Smith had enough

45

Below: *The Brooklyn National Inter-State team of 1905-06, with Jimmy Smith at far right. Bottom: According to this cartoonist at least, Smith attracted fans every bit as zealous as those of the day's other sports heroes. Below right: Brunswick's first hard rubber ball was worth showing off.*

match-game victories to his credit to be regarded as the national champion. For years he fended off challenges to this unofficial title, touring the country, whipping innumerable local hotshots on their home lanes. During the nine years of such junkets to defend his match-play title, he averaged about 207.

In 1917, Smith and Gengler toured the country together putting on exhibitions. After getting along amiably for a while on the tour, they had a falling out, which eventually led to a dramatic showdown between the two. It came in 1928, by which time both were past their prime but more than primed to settle an old score. "This was the only time Smith ever set up terms for a match," recalled Ray ("Red") Bock, who organized Smith's tours. "His only requirements were for new alleys, new three-pound six-ounce pins, the wearing of white by the

pinboys, and the use of new balls by both contestants. Smith completely outclassed Gengler, and that was the end of the Count's career."

Although Smith's reign as match king (1905-1922) was the longest ever, it was not until 1922 that an "official" match-play champion was determined, at the World Classic in Chicago. Tournament organizer Louis B. Petersen invited, among some two dozen star bowlers, Smith, hefty Mort Lindsey, Phil Wolf, whose thumb on his bowling hand had been severed at the joint ("my dumb," he called it), Hank Marino, a youngster from Chicago, and Jimmy Blouin, a transplanted Canadian, whose home base, Blue Island, Illinois, and slow, devastating curve ball earned him the nickname "the Blue Island Bomber." One of Gengler's most impressive feats had been to beat Blouin and Blouin's father on their home lanes.

Wolf had been a member of ABC championship teams in 1909 and 1920. Lindsey had also bowled for two title-winning squads and had taken the 1919 ABC all-events championship. Smith had been the all-events champ in 1911 and 1920. And Blouin had won the ABC all-events in 1909, at age 22, and the singles title in 1911.

At the World Classic, each man had to roll a five-game block against every other bowler, But to earn the title of match champion the top finisher would then have to defeat, in order, those who had finished second, third, and fourth. (Years later, Petersen admitted he hoped no one would win the title in 1922 and that a lengthy quest for this honor would give it a unique status in the world of sports. Petersen felt certain that no one would triumph in the 115-game grind and then dispose of the top three finishers.) The World Classic was to be decided not by the conventional system of total pin fall, but by the new Petersen Point System, which awarded one-fiftieth of a point for each pin, one point for every game won, and another point to the bowler who knocked down the most pins during each block.

The first phase of the tournament ended with Wolf, who had moved up from far back in the pack, with a higher average than Blouin (206.24 to 206.14) but with "the Blue Island Bomber" on top in Petersen points: 547.14 to Wolf's 535.03. Third was Lindsey, fourth Smith. Marino wound up a disappointing ninth.

In the first two matches in his quest for the

match-play title, Blouin beat Wolf and Lindsey. That meant that Blouin had to get past just one more opponent, Jimmy Smith. When they had met during the tournament, Smith had prevailed 1122-952. This time, though, they had to roll 60 games in the ultimate matchup: the longtime unofficial champion from the East against the best in the West. (None of the 24 who had started the Classic came from west of Wisconsin.) This was undoubtedly the biggest event in the history of the sport up to that date. One reporter wrote, "Bowling addicts went completely daffy, newspapers headlined it like a World Series in baseball. Thousands of fans tried every known device and invented new ones to gain admission . . . and relayed progress of the match to a milling mob outside."

Smith zipped quickly in front. Halfway through, he led by almost nine Petersen points, a comfortable margin. After 50 games, however, Blouin had trimmed Smith's lead to one-tenth of a point. Smith's fingers were bleeding, irritated by a sticky powder used by the pinboys to help them get a grip on the balls. Smith held off Blouin until the fifty-seventh game, at the end of which they were dead-

locked. Blouin kept up his surge, outscoring Smith
in the fifty-eighth 223-209. In the fifty-ninth both
rolled 223. Then came the finale. Smith rolled a
204, but was outdistanced by Blouin's 235.

Although Smith did not complain about it,
there was no doubt that his injured hand had ham-
pered him, and there were strong suspicions that to
protect their bets on Blouin, the pinboys had deliberately placed their sticky powder in the finger
holes of Smith's ball. Thereafter, a rule was passed
that at title matches pinboys had to wear white
gloves and that there had to be a supervisor behind
the pits. In making similar stipulations for his challenge match with Gengler six years later, Smith evidently remembered his misfortune only too well.

Opposite: *Jimmy Blouin, "the Blue Island Bomber," foiled Louis
B. Petersen's plans for a supreme tournament of champions when
he won Petersen's 1921 World Classic. This was supposed to be
a championship tournament so demanding that no one would win,
the better to hype the search for a truly indisputable
national champ (and the next World Classic). Blouin's win
proved a hard act to follow, and the World Classic never did:
it folded.* Above: *The Brunswick Mineralites of 1928 included
some of the biggest names in bowling in the twenties.
Standing, left to right: Chuck Collier, Harry Steers, Frank
Thoma; seated: Sykes Thoma and Frank Kartheiser.*

How the Bowling Alley Got a Bad Reputation and How It Began to Change

In a *History of Recreation/America Learns to Play*, Foster Rhea Dulles wrote of the "lure of the wicked city" during the 1890s and early 1900s, and mentioned bowling centers among the "more questionable resorts." Bowling centers were dank and small, filled with boozers and gamblers, with grime and sweat, with clouds of cigar smoke and torrents of foul language. Almost all bowling took place in alleys connected with bars, and even more than the game of billiards that had preceded it into this environment, bowling was more a social event than a competitive sport. A Chicago newspaper in the early 1900s described two of the first indoor centers: "Both were bars, and the bowling alleys were [there] to attract trade.... One got a check with each beer, and two checks entitled the drinker to bowl a game." Enticements of this sort were typical, for proprietors found it difficult to make a living off their alleys alone. By the turn of the century a solid, albeit unholy trinity had been formed: booze, billiards, and bowling.

The forerunner of what is today the Brunswick Corporation may have helped forge this union. John M. Brunswick built his first billiard table in 1845, and soon after his Cincinnati cabinet shop was formed into a company, it began making hand-crafted bars and bar fixtures. In 1884, the company began manufacturing bowling equipment. Thus, it was logical that Brunswick should tie together sales of bar, billiard, and bowling items. Former Brunswick president and board chairman R. F. Bensinger says, "They just seemed to go together naturally." And so they did, what with tavern keepers enticing customers with billiards and bowling to perk up the trade.

The worst smudge on bowling's reputation came from bookies who infiltrated bars to pick up wagers on sporting events, primarily on horse rac-

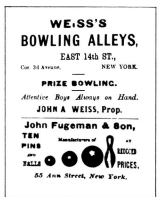

ing and billiards, but occasionally on bowling. Policing such activities was almost impossible. With bundles of money riding on more than a few tenpin matches, it was inevitable that some contests would be rigged, either through the use of illegal equipment (such as the infamous, loaded "dodo" ball), dumping, or the manipulation of pinboys.

As bowling moved indoors, often into squalid quarters, respectable men and, especially, women abandoned it. Once, there had been a conscious effort to attract women patrons, as this report from a Milwaukee newspaper of March 6, 1855, indicates:

"The ladies who passed through Burns' swinging doors took a shocked look at the joint and told the proprietor it would never do if he wanted the feminine trade. Spittoons went out, the geniune oil paintings of naked nymphs came down from behind the bar, curtains were hung and rugs laid. The help were ordered to shave at least twice a week. Signs went up asking gents to kindly refrain from profane language."

Nonetheless, by the turn of the century, the females who frequented bowling establishments resembled in breeding, elegance, and reputation

50

As these turn-of-the century advertisements indicate, bowling was only one of the pleasures pursued in the establishments that housed the alleys. The other entertainments were very often sordid, and their influence rubbed off on bowling, damaging its reputation for a long time.

FRANK SMITH'S
BowlingSaloon

307 ARCH STREET,
PHILADELPHIA.

Bagatelle, Shuffle and Revolo Boards.

Choice Wines, Liquors and Segars ; also finest
Ales and Lager Beer in the city.

the one described in a 1908 song, *Set 'Em Up In the Other Alley*:

Louie O'Malley, who worked in an alley
And spent his time setting up pins,
Loved Lena von Kohler, a fair lady bowler,
Who used to bounce pins off his shins.
She'd aim at the headpin and hit the 'pin head'
        in
The chest with a twenty-pound ball.
He'd holler, "Don't poodle, look out for my
        noodle."
Then to him she loudly would call:
"Set 'em up in the other alley, old Pally,
I'll sock 'em all in the air,

Right down the alley, old Pally, don't dally:
It's either a 'strike' or a 'spare.'
Watch the ball kiss 'em, say I couldn't miss
        'em,
I'll give those old ten pins 'a pain.'
Let 'em up, get 'em up, and when you set 'em
        up,
I'll knock 'em down again.

As the ballad progressed, Lena "rolled" Looie to the altar, then left him, taking all his "pin money." However fanciful, stories of such heroines could only have further repelled proper women from the bowling establishments.

Moralists and Prohibitionists denounced the

coarseness of life at the alleys. Yet bowlers alive today who bowled at that time insist it wasn't that bad. They assert that most gambling centered around billiards, that most drinking was done at bars rather than at the alleys, and that the presence of women who bowled, as they did in increasing numbers, helped the alleys become cleaner.

Eddie Krems, an old-time Chicago bowler and an ABC Hall of Famer, recalls, "Women didn't start bowling in Chicago until Prohibition. They followed their husbands to the alleys—or they had to stay home."

Two who followed their spouses were Mrs. Myrtle Schulte of St. Louis, who first bowled in 1917, and Mrs. Violet ("Billy") Simon of San Antonio, who started in 1921 in Minnesota. "Every week we got six couples together and bowled," Mrs. Schulte remembered. "For half a dollar a couple we could eat all we wanted—slaw, cider, soda, sandwiches—and could bowl as long as we wanted, which was usually from seven-thirty at night until about one or two in the morning. At first, the spittoons were full to the top and the places were not clean. But as more women came around, they cleaned the places up."

Mrs. Simon, one of the first female proprietors, owned the first of her eight bowling centers in 1930. "When I came to San Antonio from Minne-

Cramped, dimly lit, and poorly ventilated, bowling alleys were as aesthetically unappealing as they were of dubious moral standing. Opposite: *a subterranean alley.* Above: *Although this establishment (circa 1910) accommodated two women guests, it was clearly a male enclave, like most other alleys.*

53

sota in 1926, the German influence was strong and most of the bowling there was ninepins. I got them into tenpins. Owners made most of their money off bars, so they didn't pay much attention to their lanes. The things that got women to bowl were that the places were cleaned up, classes were held so they could learn the game, and they were made welcome. *Knowing* they were welcome was very important to women."

Dennis J. Sweeney gave women's bowling a much needed stimulus, starting the first women's leagues in 1907 in St. Louis, where he was a long-time proprietor. That same year, he received permission from the ABC to conduct the first informal national tournament for women on the same lanes that had been used by the men. The winner of that inaugural match, the ABC Ladies Championship, was Birdie Kern of St. Louis, whose father, Martin, had won the ABC singles and all-events in 1904.

Mrs. Ellen Kelly organized the first local women's bowling association in St. Louis in 1915. She also wrote to women across the country, urging them to start similar groups. In response to Kelly, "about forty" women showed up for the first "national" championships, held at Sweeney's lanes. Afterward, Sweeney convinced the contestants to begin a national organization of their own. That day, November 29, 1916, the women formed the Woman's National Bowling Congress, which later became the Women's International Bowling Congress (WIBC).

Three women bowlers who excelled early on were Addie Ruschmeyer of New York, Goldie Greenwald of Cleveland, and the aforementioned Birdie Kern. They were among the first to bowl exhibitions against men, winning often enough to earn respect for women bowlers. Greenwald rolled a 300 in one of those matches and in 1918 averaged 191 in a men's league.

On December 18, 1927, one of the most famous bowling matches in history further bolstered the claim of women to a legitimate place in the sport. Jimmy Smith came to Denver for an exhibition and consented to roll a pair of three-game matches against a rapidly improving local bowler, Mrs. Floretta McCutcheon. Smith resisted at first, explaining to her that he had never bowled against a woman and that, well, since he was regarded as the world champion and since people had come to see him bowl, he would have to "roll the very best I

The first women to return to the game left no doubt in their dress that they had come to bowl and not for other sport. Clockwise from above: Myrtle Schulte, Emma Jaeger, Birdie Humphreys—*champions all. Opposite:* St. Louis bowling team about 1910.

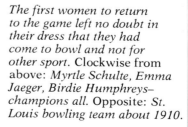

GOOD BOWLING

LESLIE'S

ILLUSTRATED WEEKLY

can." Graciously, the matronly, prematurely white-haired Mrs. Mac replied, "Well, you simply *must* do your very best." And so the world champ went against a portly, 39-year-old woman who had been bowling for a little more than two years. Smith later said, "I got the surprise of my life that night." Bowling his "very best," Smith narrowly outscored Mrs. McCutcheon in the first three-game block, 680-672. Then, as she defeated him 246-224 in the opener of the second block, Jimmy knew he was facing an extraordinary challenge. "I blinked my eyes and rolled up my sleeves," Smith admitted. In game two, Smith came out ahead 256-234, leaving both contestants with scores of 480. Surely, the pressure would now get to Mrs. Mac in the finale. It did not. She shocked Smith 224-217, winning the block 704-697. For the full six games, Smith led by one pin: 1377-1376. But the news was out that Mrs. Mac had beaten the finest bowler in the world in that second block. It even made Ripley's *Believe It or Not* feature. Jimmy Smith believed it. After his stunning loss, some suggested that Mrs. Mac might merely have been lucky. "No, she is simply the greatest bowler I have ever seen," Smith insisted.

Mrs. Mac's victory set her up for a decade of exhibition bowling. It also established her as an instant expert and led to the founding of the Mrs. McCutcheon School for Bowling Instructions. Through this school she made her most lasting contribution to the game, teaching bowling to between three and five hundred thousand women, many of whom became organizers and teachers themselves.

At the turn of the century, Chicago bowling proprietor Andrew Rohn had observed, "If proprietors endeavor to so conduct their places that businessmen may visit them, even when accompanied by wives and sweethearts, without being brought into contact with objectionable characters and without having to listen to loud and vulgar obscenities, I can see no reason for any decline [in bowling]."

In the twenties that effort began. To be sure, there were still plenty of dingy and dimly lit establishments. Pinboys were often seedy persons. And the alleys still rumbled with balls running along wooden return racks. Nonetheless, for the first time in decades the sport began to attract large numbers of women and white-collar workers. Fewer subter-

ranean alleys were built, and as the ABC stepped up its policing, fewer bookies made their headquarters at the lanes. In any event, the game boomed. In 1914, it was estimated that there were seventy-five thousand bowlers in Chicago. In 1927, a Chicago newspaper put the figure at 400,000, making it "by far the most popular sport in Chicago." Within a decade after Armistice Day, the ABC's enrollment had multiplied one hundredfold to 139,000, the WIBC's from 641 to 7,757. With its ruling bodies thriving at last and its image becoming more respectable, bowling was well on its way to becoming the most popular American game of the twentieth century.

Even as women in bowling could claim a certain stylishness (opposite right) *they provoked some predictable male condescension* (above). *Meanwhile, bowling continued to serve political cartoonists as a handy metaphor. That's Woodrow Wilson eyeing the opposition,* opposite top left, *and Teddy Roosevelt bowling it over,* opposite bottom left.

Heroes' Showcases: the All-Star and the Classic Leagues

The 1922 World Classic marked an important point in top-level competition: it ended Jimmy Smith's reign as national champion and began that of Jimmy Blouin. Yet the tournament failed to establish itself, and with its demise the match-game championship was again settled by challenge matches.

Blouin, who had a reputation for being able to gear himself up for only important matches, successfully defended his title against five challengers: Smith, Joe Falcaro, Wolf, Lindsey, and Joe Scribner. After swamping Scribner by 1,163 pins, Blouin was unchallenged for three years and retired from top-flight competition in 1926 because of ill health. He was 39 at the time and was regarded by many as the finest head-to-head bowler of all time, never having lost a prearranged match.

When Blouin ignored a challenge from Frank Kartheiser in 1926, the Chicagoan became the match-play champion. Kartheiser lost the title in 1927 to Milwaukee's Charlie Daw, who threw one of the most powerful strike balls ever, a top-spinning hook that Smith said "could climb . . . a mountain." When Marino met Daw for the title later that year, interest was so high in Milwaukee that Billy Sixty, a famous local bowler and sportswriter, did a frame-by-frame radio broadcast of the match. Daw beat Marino, but lost the title in 1928 to Adolph Carlson, a big Swede from Chicago with a three-step delivery. Before the year was over, the championship had passed on to Scribner and then to "Chesty" Joe Falcaro, who hung on to it until 1933. "Chesty Joe" billed himself as "Bowling's Undefeated World's Match Champion," a claim that irked many bowlers because Joe did not live up to his promise to "meet any bowler, anywhere, for any amount." He spurned several challenges, including repeated efforts by Sixty for a match

with Marino. Said Sixty, "Whenever I would make the challenge, Joe would say, 'Marino? Who's he? Tell him to get a reputation if he wants to bowl me.'"

In an effort to put an official stamp on the match-play title once again, the newly formed Bowling Proprietors' Association of America set up a series of eliminations to select a challenger for Falcaro. Joe Miller of Buffalo won those eliminations and was declared champion in 1933 when Falcaro was unable to bowl against him because of an injury. Otto Stein, Jr., of St. Louis defeated Miller in 1934 and then lost the next year to Marino, who retained the title until he retired briefly in 1938. He was 45 when he finally became the match king.

When Marino ended his retirement, also in 1938, it was to accept a match against the boyish-looking Ned Day, 27, the newest young dynamo in the sport. Day had left his home in Los Angeles to hone his game in the Midwest, where so many superb bowlers competed, settling first in Chicago, then Milwaukee. An extremely proper gentleman, Day was so precise in his grooming that he often carried a makeup kit. When someone at the lanes sought to shake his hand, he would often cover his hand with a towel first, ostensibly to protect his fingers. He could be a similarly meticulous bowler, particularly when his smooth, seamless delivery found the groove. This was the case as he dethroned Marino.

Three years later, in December 1941, Day still reigned as the match-game champion when the next attempt was made to supplant the challenge-match system for determining the champ. Like the World Classic, this tournament was the idea of Louis B. Petersen. This time, though, he had the support of the Bowling Proprietors' Association of

Ned Day in 1938 after winning the national match game championship from Hank Marino. Day helped the BPAA All-Star replace the chaotic system of challenge matches for determining the national champion.

America in concert with the Bowling Proprietors' Association of Greater Chicago, a sponsoring alliance that was to last until the late fifties. The two associations brought the concept to Arch Ward, the Chicago *Tribune's* sports editor, whose credits included baseball's All-Star Game. Ward persuaded his paper to sponsor the new event, and the first All-Star soon became the most prestigious bowling tournament in the country.

It gained preeminence quickly partly because it was so demanding. At the start it ran for eight days, with each bowler rolling 64 games. Later it expanded to as many as 100 games for the men and 77 for the women. Of these games, 64 for the men and 32 for the women were packed into the last four days of head-to-head play. In the locker room between matches, bowlers would care for their raw thumbs, seek massages and other treatments from trainers, even grab a catnap. The All-Star was nothing short of an endurance contest.

A few hours after the first All-Star began, at Chicago's Coliseum, it almost ended, when the news arrived that Pearl Harbor had been bombed. The spectators sat stunned after the announcement, then began to leave the arena. Tournament officials considered canceling the tournament but finally decided to proceed. Johnny ("the General") Crimmins won it by soundly defeating his closest challenger, Joe Norris. When Day agreed to defend his match-game title against Crimmins, the new

All-Star champ, before the next year's tournament, the stage was set for one of the most controversial of all match-play confrontations.

While the rest of the field rolled the preliminary rounds of the second All-Star, Crimmins and Day met in a 90-game tussle. Trailing from the outset, Crimmins waited until the final five-game block to make his move, trying to overcome Day's seven-point Petersen lead. Crimmins opened with eight strikes and drubbed Day, 269-185, in the first game. With 13 strikes and 9 spares in the next two games, Crimmins won two more times, 224-219 and 227-171. That left him only slightly more than a point behind Day. Then, two strikes in the tenth frame enabled Crimmins to win the fourth game, 201-188. Thus, after 89 games, he had forged in front, by a little more than a point. But suddenly, he allowed the title to slip away. Day marked in every frame of the ninetieth game and won it, 203-178. Crimmins still led by 30 pins for the entire event, but Day had won on Petersen points: 399.49 to 398.29. Each man had won 45 games, but the Petersen system gave Day an extra point in the third block, in which he lost on games but had a higher pinfall. By a quirk in the system, Day was still the match-game champion.

Now Day gave the All-Star the prestige it needed to become the premier event in the sport. He relinquished the match-game crown he had just successfully defended, agreeing that the winner of the 1942 All-Star be declared the champion. It was a magnanimous gesture, and a costly one. Although both Day and the bitterly disappointed Crimmins were seeded in the 12-man finals, the ultimate victor was Connie Schwoegler, a 6-foot 3-inch, 225-pounder from Madison, Wisconsin, who had never won a major title.

Day, who had defended, then relinquished, then failed to retain the title in 1942, won it right back at the 1943 All-Star by outclassing Chicago's Paul Krumske. Despite the win, the much-challenged Day could not relax. The All-Star championship had yet to make the challenge match obsolete, and Day soon faced still another such match from Krumske.

"In those days, the runnerup had the privilege of challenging the All-Star winner within a year to try to take away his title," Krumske recalled. "I went a long time without picking up my option. Then Louie Petersen urged me to go after Day. I

Opposite left: *Johnny Crimmins, winner of the first All-Star, then loser of a challenge match to Day, though he had a higher pinfall.* Opposite right: *Hank Marino, match-game champion in the thirties, was still going strong in the forties, when he was in his fifties.* Above: *Marie Warmbier was the queen of women's bowling in the thirties.*

. AMERICAN .
BOWLING CONGRESS CHICAGO
1929

DUFFY
FLORALS
CHICAGO

told him there were three reasons why I hadn't done so: one, I needed to put up one thousand dollars for such a match; two, I had a heart condition and didn't think I could bowl eighty games, which [were the terms] Day liked to have; and three, I didn't think I could beat Day. Louie said he'd take care of things. He did. A sixty-game match was set up, the first half in Chicago and the second at Day's place in West Allis, Wisconsin. He had his lanes tricked up. Day threw as big a hook as anyone. On lane one at his place, he would bowl from the far left as if he were going to throw his big hook. But his ball would do nothing but slide until it got near the headpin and then it would actually fade back into the pocket. He either got a strike or a split. I bowled as far to the right as Day did to the left. Lane two wasn't so bad. It was real tight, but you could make the ball hook.

"In the tenth frame of the fifty-seventh game, I needed a strike to shut out Day. If I got that strike, Day would need three 300s and I would have to roll about 120 each game for him to beat me. Fans were jammed in behind us and along both lanes in special bleachers from the foul line all the way to the pits. I picked up my ball in the tenth and held it in my left hand. To dry my right thumb, I had a habit of rubbing it against my pants. Finally some lady yelled, 'Thirty-four, thirty-five, thirty-six—*throw the ball!*' I put the ball down and glared at her. They said I only rubbed my thumb twelve times when I finally got up again. I got my strike and then said to the woman, 'Lady, that was for you.' "

So ended the brilliant, if somewhat confusing, reign of Ned Day. The option of the All-Star runner-up to challenge the winner, as Krumske had Day, was soon rescinded. Thereafter the All-Star champ could claim the match-game title with universal acceptance. Half a century after the first ABC tournament, a quarter century after the World Classic Invitational, bowling at last had an orderly procedure for determining its individual champion.

Like the individual match-game title, the national team championship was for years settled by challenges. One of the most dominant of the early teams, the Duffy Florals of Chicago, held the undisputed but unofficial championship for years, until 1929, when they ran into Detroit's Palace Recreation outfit. It was a matchup of some of the greatest bowlers of the day: the Duffy Florals' Eddie

Bowling was glamorous in the thirties, and the stars of the sport associated with the other celebrities of the day. Top: *Paul Krumske and Red Faber;* above: *Eddie Krems with John Barrymore.* Opposite *(standing, left to right): Krems, Dom DeVito, Marino; (seated): Bill Brennan and Joe Fliger.*

63

Krems, Hank Marino, Frank Kartheiser, Dom De-Vito, and Joe Fliger against the young Detroit Palace squad of Joe Norris, Bill North, Ernie Hartman, Walter Reppenhagen, and Johnny Crimmins. A home-and-home match, as tradition decreed, this one began with 12 games in Detroit, where the Palace team built a 400-pin lead. A week later, the two teams squared off in Chicago, where the Palace players' new all-white uniforms quickly earned them the nickname "Street Cleaners" from the heckling fans. Clean up they did, sweeping the Florals and the championship.

During the thirties, Marino joined with Billy Sixty, Charlie Daw, and other Milwaukeeans to form a Heil Products squad that held the title for three years. Then Hermann's Undertakers of St. Louis took command, holding the title from 1938 to 1942. On January 27, 1937, this team rolled a three-game set in which no man scored less than 222: 1,261, 1,211, 1,325—a record 3,797.

With the repeal of Prohibition, in 1933, beer manufacturers began backing teams, some of them among the finest in the game's history. Stroh's beer pioneered the practice of assuring bowlers a sufficient income from exhibitions so that they could devote most of their time to the game. Cream-colored flannel uniforms became one of the trademarks of this Detroit-based group, which took the ABC and national match titles during its first season, 1933-34. The R. J. Reynolds Tobacco Company offered the team a reported $50,000 to tour the country promoting Camel cigarettes, but the bowlers rejected the offer and remained with Stroh's.

These teams and their competitors came from bowling's answer to baseball's farm system, the classic leagues. In 1932, the Chicago proprietors sensed that they could stimulate interest in bowling (and therefore their businesses) by assembling the best local bowlers in a special league. The idea spread to other cities, and before long there were intercity matches between All-Star squads drawn from each city's classic leagues.

Krumske, one of many great alumni of Chicago's Classic League and in 1951 voted Chicago's Bowler of the Half Century, recalls, "Men came from all over the country to Chicago to try to join the league. I won the high individual average seven or eight times, the most of anybody. And my teams must have won about fifteen league championships. I belonged to lots of teams: Bowlers Aid, Eidelweiss, Baby Ruth, Pabst, Meister Brau. Schlitz beer had a team in the league, so I joined it. When Meister Brau reorganized, I became a member. For about eighteen years I was captain, and we won many championships.

"When ABC came out with its 'alley man' rule, it caused a problem. That rule said a team could not have more than one man who earned more than half his income from bowling. At that time I worked for Bowling and Billiard Supplies. Under the new rule that meant I was considered a pro, even though I didn't spend as much time bowling as some other men. Another member of our Pabst team affected by this rule was Herb Freitag, the manager of some bowling lanes, so we were over the limit. Well, Eddie Krems was our captain and he was in a quandary. I told Eddie, 'I'll take you off the hook. I'll resign from the team.' That made headlines across eight columns in the Chicago papers."

In the classic leagues for teams, in the All-Star tournament for individuals, bowling now had a competitive structure for its top performers that added both to their appeal and to the appeal of the game. People paid to see the stars perform in these contests, but more importantly, they followed their exploits through the media and followed their lead by becoming more proficient and more enthusiastic bowlers themselves. Bowling had always had its heroes; now it was starting to market them.

There was one very notable exception—a 5-foot 6-inch, 180-pound, barrel-chested, bow-legged dynamo who marketed himself not only through the classic leagues and the match-play challenges. He was Andy Varipapa, a splendid showman and athlete, whose trick bowling exhibitions made him "the greatest one-man bowling show on earth," as he billed himself. With a twist of his powerful wrist he threw a "boomerang ball," which skittered down the lane and then came right back to him. He converted 4-6 and 7-9-10 leaves with aplomb. And in his most famous feat, he rolled two balls simultaneously—one with each hand—to convert either the 7-10 split or what he called the "double pinochle"—the 4-7 *and* the 6-10. Many years later, he was still astounding people with his bowling skills. In 1969, at age 78, he began bowling left-handed when his right arm and wrist began to bother him. Within two years he was averaging 180.

With Andy Varipapa leading the way, bowling went to the movies in 1934, in Strikes and Spares, starring Varipapa, Sally McKee, and Buster Brodie (left and above left). A successful competitor but an even more successful showman, Varipapa made his reputation as the master of the trick shot. At the mellow age of 78, he added left-handed bowling to his repertoire (above right).

The Start of Something Big

Disgusted with pinboys who were ill-kempt, disorderly, foul-mouthed, and late or absent, a Pearl River, New York, proprietor named George Bickerle one day found himself entertaining the fantasy of a machine that could replace those rowdies. In 1931, Bickerle mentioned the possibility to an engineer who bowled at his establishment, Gottfried ("Fred") Schmidt. Recognizing that the local Dexter Folder Company, where Schmidt worked, used suction for feeding paper through its machines, Bickerle wondered if a similar principle could be used for spotting pins. Schmidt thought it could.

It was in an abandoned turkey house on the Pearl River farm of Fred Sandhage, a machinist assisting in the venture, that Schmidt assembled the first model of this improbable machine, a laughably crude contraption outfitted with lamp shades for spotting pins and flower pots for respotting them. In 1936, encouraged by early tests of the machine, Schmidt sought out Robert E. Kennedy of Brunswick, who passed on details of Schmidt's project to company officials. They showed no interest; Brunswick had tried for years to develop such a machine and had given up.

In 1937, Kennedy left Brunswick for another job and looked up Schmidt, who had all but forgotten about his machine. Kennedy contacted Morehead Patterson, then vice-president of the little-known American Machine & Foundry Company (AMF). Patterson surveyed the lamp shades, flower pots, and turkey house and, inventor that he himself was, concluded that here was a machine that with proper refinement would revolutionize bowling. AMF put its experts to work on the project.

In the meantime, the industry pushed ahead on other fronts. In January 1936, while still at Brunswick, Kennedy had found himself reporting to company headquarters in Chicago that for the fifth straight week the New York division, of which he was in charge, had repossessed more bowling lanes than it had sold. The Depression had struck, and though in general bowling held up better than most businesses, it had yet to banish the back-alley taint that kept some people away. Kennedy decided the time had come to redesign bowling houses to project the image of respectability the game sought. Soon, new houses were built and old ones remodeled with seats (in place of wooden benches), settees, brighter lighting, and more colorful wall designs. As befitted *its* image, Hollywood boasted one of the fanciest bowling setups in the late thirties. The studio where Al Jolson made the first talking motion picture, Warner Brothers' Studio One, was converted into a 52-lane house and rechristened Sunset Lanes.

While the exploits of the Days, Krumskes, Marinos, and Varipapas publicized the game at its highest levels, the growing grassroots commanded attention of their own. As teams and leagues sprang up and lanes were installed in hundreds of social clubs, churches, and YMCAs, the game was depicted in cartoons and on the covers of *The Saturday Evening Post, Collier's, Esquire,* and even *The Literary Review.* "The sport got tremendous space in the newspapers," said Billy Sixty. "Every Sunday the [Milwaukee] *Journal* carried a full page of league scores and standings."

Then came World War II, and still another challenge to the game's continued growth. Congress contemplated a 20 percent tax on bowling but relented when John Canelli, an ABC director, argued persuasively that such a tax would both put proprietors out of business and deprive millions of Americans of a much-needed recreational outlet. Taking the argument to its logical conclusion, the

The automatic pinspotter was not a new idea (opposite top). The first workable design for a fully automatic model was hatched in the late thirties, in an abandoned turkey house, in front of which inventor Fred Schmidt and patron Morehead Patterson (of AMF) later posed (opposite bottom).

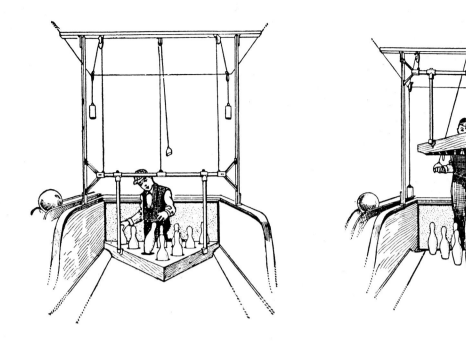

Although the big change in bowling interiors would not come until after the automatic pinspotter, bowling houses began to modernize as early as the thirties. Hard-backed benches and other stolid wooden fixtures (opposite top) gave way to sleeker, upholstered furnishings (opposite bottom). San Diego's Tower Bowl (left and below) opted for the streamline look of art deco.

bowling industry quickly realized that because it was a recreational outlet, the game could, in fact, assist the war effort by bolstering workers' morale. Soon a massive program was begun to convince employers, primarily factory owners, to sponsor teams in industrial leagues. Committees were formed to promote the game at plants and offices, and the new National Bowling Council (NBC), an umbrella organization for the various bowling groups, deluged any interested party with instructional literature.

Special tournaments and matches were set up to raise funds for the Community War Chest, War Bond Drives, the Red Cross, and the USO. After some of those events, the contestants donated blood. Substantial financial contributions were given to the Bowlers Victory Legion, founded in 1942 to provide recreational and other equipment for men and women in the armed services (and still active today). The WIBCers backed several extensive fundraising campaigns, the slogan for the first of which was: "Our answer to bombs—a bomber." The initial drive brought in more than $100,000, and on March 23, 1943, a bomber christened *Miss WIBC* was presented to the U.S. Army Air Force. That done, the women embarked upon another project, one they felt would reflect a more "humane, rather than destructive" attitude. Their Wings of Mercy program netted $341,543.25 for the purchase of an ambulance and three ambulance planes.

Before the war was over, it was evident that bowlers had done a lot of fundraising and a lot of bowling. The well-organized wartime teams and leagues kept many people in contact with the sport (and each other) and recruited newcomers, particularly women. The WIBC almost doubled its membership during the war—to 252,540.

In 1940, there were 12 million bowlers in America. By 1946, the number had risen to 16 million and by 1948, at the start of the postwar surge, to 20 million. *Fortune* and *Life* magazines marveled at this rapid growth. In 1949, the New York *Times* reported in some wonderment that there were 58 bowling establishments in Manhattan, 7 "advertising twenty-four-hour service so waiters, cab drivers, bartenders, and show people can drop in on the way home."

Fashionable Vassar College added bowling to its intramural collegiate sports program. President Harry S. Truman had two lanes installed in the White House basement. (They have since been moved across the street.)

At long last, the back-alley image was banished, but it was just the start. All the building and remodeling, the new teams and leagues, the entire "make bowling respectable" campaign, impressive as the progress was, paled when compared to the effects of the technological innovation that had first begun in the Pearl River, New York, turkey house in the early thirties. For now, at last, the Pinspotter, as AMF hailed its new marvel, was ready. Just as Morehead Patterson had predicted, bowling was about to be revolutionized.

The Second World War brought women bowlers to the support of the fighting forces (above) *and more women to bowling* (opposite bottom). *The bowling industry shrewdly realized that the game could provide a much-needed recreational outlet for Americans caught up in the war effort, and the more aggressive promoters pushed it as positively patriotic as well* (opposite top and middle).

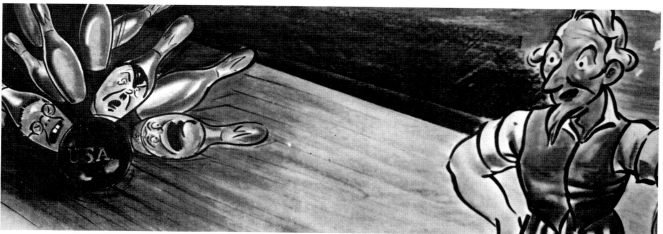

The Pinspotter Revolution

In 1945, Robert E. Kennedy, formerly of Brunswick, came to AMF to set up marketing arrangements for the company's new Pinspotter division. In March 1946, during the ABC tournament in Buffalo, the first two Pinspotters were unveiled. There was no room for them at the tournament site, so Kennedy rented a portion of a huge garage across the street, where bowlers could test the machines for themselves, rolling on lanes on which the Pinspotters had been installed. Within six weeks almost fifty thousand people came to see these "electro-mechanical devices" in action. Each machine stood 7 feet 9 inches tall, weighed more than two tons, and contained more than thirteen hundred parts, including several motors and a huge control box crammed with so many wires that it looked like a vat of spaghetti. There were "Pindicators" on the front of each machine, flashing an "X" for a strike, a "/" for a spare. The Pindicators also showed whether a shot was the first or second of a frame, and signaled which pins were left standing after the first ball.

It took 17 seconds for the first Pinspotters to complete each cycle—sweeping dead wood away, respotting the pins, and returning the ball to the bowler. Despite the din and malfunctioning of the early models, bowlers and proprietors were enamored of them. Contracts for more than 10,000 were drawn up, with a $1,000 down payment on each.

In August 1951, 12 units of a refined model were installed at Don Peltier's Bowl-O-Drome in Mt. Clemens, Michigan—the first time a bowling center was operated without pinboys. These Pinspotters had been reduced to 5 feet 2 inches, weighed closer to one ton than two, and contained a miniaturized control box. They functioned so well that mass production was begun immediately.

On August 15, 1952, Ollie Holmes's 16-lane Farragut Pool Lanes in Brooklyn, New York, became the first center equipped with the factory models. Automated bowling had begun in earnest.

As AMF struggled to produce enough machines to meet the demand, the company plunged headlong into the bowling business. In 1953, it purchased the National Bowling and Billiard Supply Company of Chicago, which permitted it to furnish a complete line of bowling equipment. Brunswick, according to some sources nearly ruined by its lack of an automatic pinspotter, began a crash program to develop one.

In the December 12, 1955, issue of *Sports Illustrated*, Victor Kalman described the immediate impact of the automatic pinsetter. "Many alleys [had been] forced to operate part time because [pinboys] were not available," Kalman wrote. "With 'automatics' an establishment [could] operate 24 hours a day, 365 days a year—and many did. . . .

"Machines, or the promise of them in the near future, enabled businesspeople to invest with confidence in plush surburban palaces far from the pinboy labor market but with *space*—space for parking and space for spectators, neither of which the high-rental city centers could duplicate. The boom in suburbia was on. . . . Almost overnight, bowling had been transformed from a small-time operation run by individuals into big business. . . . The alleys, in ill-repute little more than a generation ago, have become recreational centers for entire communities."

By mid-1955 there were 3,711 more bowling houses than on VJ Day, a 62 percent increase in a decade. Some of the new establishments were lavish. North Kansas City Bowl had an art gallery and an aviary. Others had swimming pools, dance bands, waterfalls, fountains, indoor miniature golf

The first automatic pinspotter model, crude and cumbersome in comparison to today's machines, was nonetheless an impressive and dramatic mechanical advance, which quickly and drastically changed the nature of the game.

courses, and beauty parlors. In 1955, shortly after Anton ("Tony") Vogel opened his $1.5 million 50-lane Bowlero in Clifton, New Jersey, the New York *Daily News* raved, "It's a gasser—3½ acres of building, 4½ of parking lots, a coffee shop, a cocktail lounge, a dining room worthy of a Miami Beach hotel."

Suddenly, bowling was more than respectable—it was stylish. And so, at long last, it attracted women en masse. "'You ask what women want,' Vogel said. 'It's class, the best. I spent months selecting the right colors and materials for the drapes, rugs, chairs, paneling and so on. . . . Why? Well, I'm open around the clock and handle 3,000 bowlers every day. Forty percent are women. Without them I wouldn't be in business.' "

To take advantage of housewives' leisure time, proprietors offered free games and lessons, and they hired telephone callers to interest women in the other attractions of the lanes, such as the nurseries and playrooms for their children. Women responded by forming leagues as never before: breakfast leagues, luncheon leagues, afternoon leagues, night leagues. In the 10-year period 1945-1955, WIBC leagues tripled to 22,482. "When you bowl now, you feel like you're *really* going out," one woman summed up to a *Life* reporter.

Another sizable part of bowling's new constituency was the teenagers, who discovered bowling centers to be ideal hangouts. They gathered to munch snacks, play the pinball machines, and, almost incidentally, try some bowling, an activity that did not strain their modest finances. Cities quickly did away with bans against teenagers in bowling establishments.

Appealing to women as well as men, to children as well as adults, bowling sold itself most of all as a family sport—the perfect pitch to a country imbued with the mission of family-rearing. Father, mother, and children, each of whom bowled with friends, also bowled with each other, as bowling became a ritual of American family life.

While the automatic pinspotter brought bowling within the reach of everyone, another technological innovation, television, publicized the sport by making it literally a game show. Two staples of American postwar leisure time, television and bowling, made a dynamic combination.

The duo's debut came in 1947, largely through the efforts of Pat McDonough, now publisher of

When at the 1946 ABC tournament AMF unveiled its mechanical marvel, and magic triangle "pindicator" to boot (top), everybody wanted to see how it worked (above). Opposite: While the crowd surrounded the demonstration model pinspotter, the pinboys worked across the street, surely aware that their days were numbered.

Sports Reporter, a New Jersey newspaper devoted to the game. The first show, from Lew Markus's Capitol Health Center on Broadway and 53rd Street in Manhattan, devoted most of its time to a mixed doubles match between two men, Tony Sparando and Marty Cassio, and two women, Mickey Michaels and Ann Sabolowski. To fill out the hour, Joe Falcaro performed trick shots and gave some bowling tips to master of ceremonies Win Elliot. As the show wound to a close, Elliot rolled one ball just for fun and provided the perfect ending with a strike.

From such tentative beginnings came some classic television fare of the fifties. "Championship Bowling," with its *sotto voce* announcer, "Whispering" Joe Wilson, made the fifth and sixth lanes at the Faetz and Niesen center on Chicago's North Side two of the most famous lanes in the country. The program began in 1953 and lasted through various alterations into the sixties.

On "Make That Spare," another long-running show, two contestants shot at five spares, each of which had a specific point value: 25 points each for the 2-4-5-8 and the 1-2-4-7, 50 points each for the 4-5 and the 1-2-4-10, and 100 points for the last one, the 5-7. The bowler with the highest total at the end of the show earned $1,000 and a chance to "break the bank" by converting the 6-7-8-10.

On "Jackpot Bowling," two well-known bowlers each rolled nine balls, always at a full rack. The one who made more strikes won $1,000. And anyone who tossed six strikes in a row won the jackpot, which started at $5,000 and rose by $1,000 each week that no one won it. Andy Varipapa outdid everyone on this show by striking nine times in a row. But the biggest jackpot, $75,000, went to Therman Gibson, on New Year's Day, 1961.

"I told my wife Eloise that I would call her if I won the jackpot," Gibson remembers. "Eloise was sitting home in Detroit with my two daughters. . . . Normally, the show was put on tape, so we'd bowl on the coast at five-thirty in the afternoon and my wife would see the show in Detroit at ten-thirty, when the tape was put on TV. I had promised to call Eloise *right away* if I ever won. This time, however, one of the announcers had to do the Rose Bowl game, so the show went out live coast to coast. Since Eloise didn't receive any call and assumed the show was taped, she also assumed I didn't win. She and the girls sat there watching,

and after I rolled the eleventh strike in a row she turned to the girls and said, 'Kids, now don't get excited, because your father misses this last strike and doesn't win the seventy-five thousand dollars.' Well, all of them sat there knowing I wouldn't make it. When I did, they all jumped around the room screaming and hugging one another."

On January 1, 1958, the New York *Times* reported, "Tenpin enthusiasts maintain that last year television devoted more time—9,000 hours—to bowling than to any other sport. Chicago had seven programs a week, while New York ran four and De-troit three." Television made the top bowlers household names across the country. And, as if to herald this new era of bowling, the game had a new superstar, whose unique style and prodigious achievements lured America to bowling much as Arnold Palmer would attract millions to golf a few years later. While the automatic pinspotter brought bowling to suburbia, and television brought it into the living room, Don Carter, as much as anyone, brought America down to the lanes.

The automatic pinspotter allowed bowling to follow America in its move to suburbia. Before long the game was as stylishly upper middle class as TV's Ozzie and Harriet (above left and right). Opposite: Clean-cut kids, too, became bowlers.

Carter and Company

It was not as if Don Carter filled a vacuum. On the contrary, there were a host of star bowlers and star bowling performances to fill the spotlight. In 1946, for example, 55-year-old Andy Varipapa won the All-Star—the oldest winner ever, and he did it the year the format was expanded to a grueling 100 games. In 1947, Varipapa became the first to win two All-Stars in a row, surviving a harrowing finish when Joe Wilman, who needed a strike in the final frame to win, made a solid pocket hit that unaccountably left the 10-pin. Junie McMahon became the second to win two All-Stars, triumphing in 1949 and 1951.

In January 1955, when Carter was in his prime, two other stars, Cleveland's Steve Nagy and cigar-chomping Ed Lubanski of Detroit, grabbed the headlines with one of the most exciting All-Star contests of the decade. Nagy was so sure he would not make it to the finals that he phoned his wife to tell her he was heading home. But he managed to tie Graz Castellano for the last spot in the finals, necessitating a six-game rolloff, starting at 2 A.M. Three hours later, Nagy's wife got another call: "Hop in the car. I'm in the finals."

It came down to a four-game contest, with Nagy needing to win either all four or at least three by a huge margin (such were the dictates of the Petersen Scoring System). Lubanski began the first game with three strikes and needed only a spare in the tenth to clinch it and, it seemed, the title as well. But his ball did not hook properly, and he was left with a wide split, which he failed to convert. Nagy edged him, 199-190. Missed spares and 7-10 splits haunted Lubanski during the next three games. Nagy won them all, clinching the championship with a strike in the ninth frame of the last contest.

An even closer finish highlighted the December 1955 All-Star. (Because of scheduling problems there were two All-Stars in 1955, none in 1953 and 1957.) Like Lubanski, Wilman missed a decisive tenth-frame spare in the last game of his contest with Bill Lillard. As the ball skimmed past the headpin of a 1-2-10 washout, Wilman became a runnerup for the third time, losing to Lillard by only eight pins.

These heroes and heroics kept the game in the sports limelight in the heady postwar years. Don Carter added the luster of a superstar.

For starters, the "St. Louis Shuffler" duplicated Varipapa's feat of winning back-to-back All-Stars, outdistancing Lubanski in 1952 and Lillard in 1954. Then Carter won consecutive All-Stars *again*, in 1956 and 1958, each time with a dramatic finishing charge. In 1956, he stormed past another St. Louis bowler, Dick Weber, who had led the qualifying rounds. In the 1958 event, Carter made an incredible comeback after barely surviving the semifinals, in which he placed forty-second among 46 qualifiers. He then blitzed his way through the finals, winning 40 of his 64 matches and finishing with a composite average of 213.72, at the time the highest ever in the All-Star.

Carter's mastery made headlines across the nation. When the Shuffler had a chance at a record third-straight title in the first of the 1955 All-Stars, the media saturated the tournament with coverage. All three wire services, 40 newspapers, seven magazines, three radio stations, and a television station came to report the event. But luck was not with Carter. Despite having the highest pinfall during the finals, he had to struggle to finish third, undone by opponents who beat his 230s with 240s, his 240s with 250s.

If Carter had a peer in his success at top-level bowling, it was a woman, Mrs. Marion Ladewig,

Left: *Judged by no more than the high-powered company they kept, Don Carter and Marion Ladewig were true superstars. This picture, taken at the 1954 All-Star, brought together (standing, from left to right): Andy Varipapa, Connie Schwoegler, Ned Day (who seems to have borrowed one of Buddy Bomar's shirts), Bomar, Dick Hoover, and Junie McMahon, and (seated, left to right): Joe Wilman, Shirley Garms, Ladewig, and Carter. Below: Varipapa after winning his second straight All-Star, in 1948.*

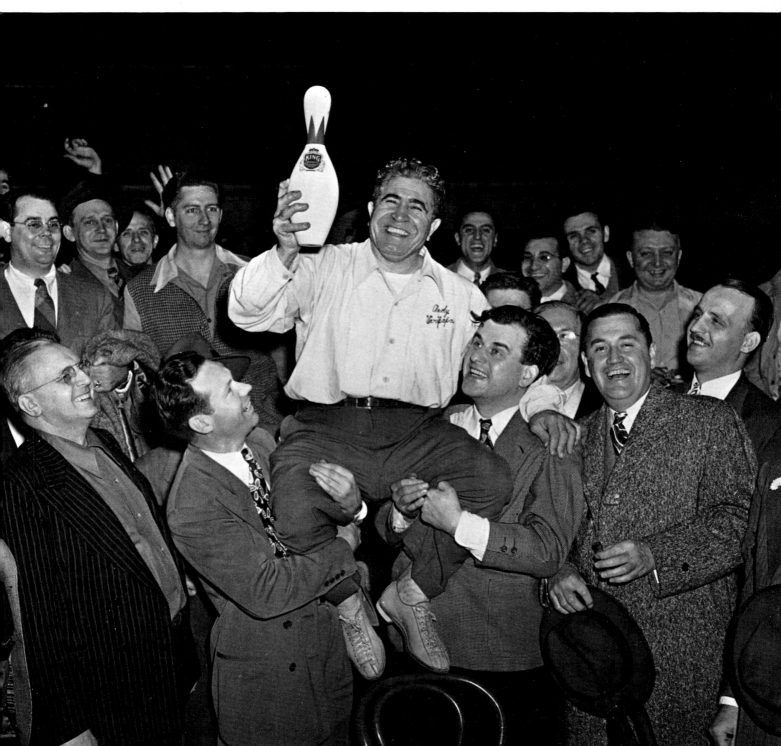

who ruled women's bowling at the time even more dominantly than Carter did men's. Ladewig won the first five All-Stars in which the women rolled (1949-1954), scoring overwhelming victories each time. Her 211.46 average in 1951 remained an All-Star high for more than two decades. Overcome by the torturous All-Star grind, she announced that the January 1955 event would be her last All-Star. She finished third, after a late spurt brought her from fifth place to second behind the new champ, 4-foot 11-inch, 130-pound Sylvia Wene of Philadelphia, who had finished second twice in the previous three years. (Miss Wene's greatest moment would come at the 1960 All-Star, when she held off Ladewig's late surge, became the first woman to bowl a 300 game in an All-Star, and won by 37 pins.)

In December 1955, ignoring her earlier protestations, Mrs. Ladewig competed in the next All-Star and finished fourth. That made two All-Stars in a row that she had *not* won, a situation she promptly corrected in 1956 with an easy victory. She lost narrowly to Merle Matthews in 1958 but then won her seventh All-Star the next year with a high-scoring finish.

After having held the All-Star in Chicago for 16 years, the BPAA announced that starting in 1957 it would take the tournament on the road. This irked the Bowling Proprietors' Association of Greater Chicago, erstwhile partners in the show, and the Chicago group promptly upstaged the BPAA and its national tournament by sponsoring a tournament "for the match-game bowling championship of the *world*." This World's Invitational tournament caught on instantly, and rivaled the All-Star.

Now Carter and Ladewig had two tournaments to dominate. Carter won five of the first six World's Invitationals (1957, 1959-1962) and finished second to Lubanski in the other. Ladewig did not sweep through the World's as she had the All-Star, but she did finish first at the 1957 opener. And in 1963, in a glorious climax to her career, she won both the World's and the All-Star, the latter her eighth such title (after having supposedly retired from All-Star competition eight years before). She finally retired in 1964, but not before yet another World's title.

While Carter and Ladewig were scaling new heights of individual achievements, team bowling flourished as never before. The splendid squads of the classic leagues now included not only the best of the local talent but bowlers recruited from other cities as well.

More than anyone, Harry Daumit, a Chicago cosmetics manufacturer, institutionalized the practice of recruiting. He paid travel expenses for bowlers who came to join his clubs, provided some with jobs in his company, and lined up others with work elsewhere in the Chicago area. To protect Chicagoans, Daumit instructed his team captain, Buddy Bomar, not to raid local teams. He needn't have worried. Aided by Mort Luby, Sr., of *Bowlers Journal* (not to be confused with *The Bowlers Journal* of the United Bowling Clubs), Bomar gathered a talented group of imports: Day from Milwaukee, Eddie Kawolics from Cleveland, Joe Kristof from Toledo, and Lee Braymiller from Buffalo. With Chicagoans Eddie Brosius and Bomar himself, this Daumit-sponsored team dethroned Paul Krumske's Meister Braus, who had won the team match-play title in 1946. Bomar's crews then held off three challengers for the title.

In a confession of sorts, Bomar revealed how his team upset the Meister Braus:

"When we were getting ready to meet the Meister Braus for the championship, we didn't have any home alleys we could use," Bomar recalls. "Leo Faetz said to me, 'I'll tell you a pair of lanes you'll love—nine and ten at Samuelson's.' Ned Day and I tried 'em. Faetz was right; we loved 'em. For all the matches I rolled there I averaged something like 263.

"Remember, this was a home-and-home match. In those days that meant *home-and-home*, and you were expected to fix up your lanes to suit yourself or your team. In those days, we bowled on shellac and they'd put some oil on top of that to condition the lanes. We never tricked up our lanes. What we did do was take advantage of the shellac. We *absolutely froze it*. The night before the match at Samuelson's, we opened every window in the place wide and cut off all the heat. Then we practiced in sweaters and sweat suits so we could learn how the balls would react on the frozen lanes. We kept the place as cold as we could by leaving the windows open all night and the heat off, and by not allowing the fans in until half an hour before the afternoon

The king and queen in action at the 1961 World's Invitational (top and left) and celebrating their victories together (above). Carter among the men and Ladewig among the women each won more All-Stars and more World's Invitationals—the two most prestigious titles of the day—than did any other bowler.

match. The Meister Braus couldn't figure out what was going on. You had to have oil on the alley for it to be slick. They looked at their bowling balls and noticed there wasn't any oil on 'em, but they still couldn't figure out what we had done. As soon as we finished bowling one block, we opened all the windows to freeze the lanes again.''

Resourceful man that he was, when Daumit dropped his sponsorship Bomar moved on to other teams—Tavern Pale, Jockey-Cooper, Falstaff, and Munsingwear—ever ready to strengthen his lineup with high-powered imports. Bomar brought in Ray Bluth from St. Louis, Lillard from Fort Worth, Earl Johnson from Tacoma, and Stan Gifford from Oregon.

As they had since the classic leagues' inception in the early thirties, breweries often sponsored many of the big teams. The E&Bs (Eckhardt and Becker brewers) plunged into big-time competition in 1944 and continued for eight years until they were taken over by Pfeiffer. Every member of the 1951 E&B lineup became an ABC Hall of Famer: Bill Bunetta, Fred Bujack, Lou Sielaff, George Young, Therman Gibson, and Chuck O'Donnell.

Others who rolled for Pfeiffer and were later enshrined were Nagy, Carter, Lillard, Lubanski, and Joe Joseph. As the E&Bs, the team snared its first national match-game championship in 1945 and its second four years later by defeating Bomar's Tavern Pales.

The most dramatic of those title defenses came in 1952 against Krumske's King Louie team. Going into the last three-game block, at Detroit's Palm Beach Recreation, King Louie led by 207 pins, having come back strongly after the E&Bs had outrolled them at home. But then the champs put on a rally of their own. Twenty-five times during the final game the lead switched hands. In the end it came down to the two anchormen, Bujack and Krumske. Bujack left himself an 8-10 split. Krumske finished with a strike. "Final" score: a tie. Happily for E&B fans, who snapped up tickets to the next day's four-game rolloff almost instantly, the home team prevailed in the extra session, by 275 pins.

The biggest of the big teams was assembled in 1954, when Jerome ("Whitey") Harris, a St. Louis policeman, went to the Budweiser people to ask for their sponsorship. They agreed, on the condition

Four of the big teams in the fifties, the big-team era—left, the 1951 E & Bs (left to right): Lou Sielaff, Therman Gibson, Bill Bunetta, Fred Bujack, and George Young; below left, the 1957 Falstaffs: Stan Gifford, Ned Day, Earl Johnson, Buddy Bomar, and Bill Lillard; opposite, the 1959 Pfeiffers: Bob Hitt, Billy Golembiewski, Joe Joseph, Bob Kwolek, and Ed Lubanski; below, perhaps the greatest team of all-time, the 1958 Budweisers (standing left to right): Bill Lillard, Ray Bluth, Dick Weber, Tom Hennessey; seated: Chuck O'Donnell, captain Pat Patterson, and Don Carter.

that he could lure Don Carter away from the Pfeiffers. Carter succumbed, and with the king of bowling on board and the king of beers paying the bills, everything else fell into place. Harris's original roster read: Carter, Bluth, Billy Welu, Pat Patterson, and Don McClaren. To that imposing array of bowlers he added Dick Weber in 1955, and Tom Hennessey in 1956. Five times during the seven years of Budweiser sponsorship the Buds had the highest league series average. They won the national match-game crown four times. In short, they forged a dynasty.

On March 12, 1958, 21 years after Hermann's Undertakers had rolled their record three-game block of 3,797, the Buds surpassed that mark, averaging 257 per man for a 3,858 total. Their greatest moment, however, may well have come in 1956, when they won the national match-game title against the Stroh's in St. Louis. At the start of the showdown, all the Buds were ailing: Weber with a cracked thumb, Carter a badly swollen knee, Patterson a hernia, Welu arm and back troubles, and

Bluth a bad shoulder. Adversity seemed to bring out the best in them. Averaging almost 219 per man, they built a 247-pin edge at home and survived in Detroit by a final margin of 29 pins.

Officials of the Falstaff brewery in St. Louis used to say, "The Buds get all the publicity, but we sell the beer." As it happened, Falstaff did outsell Budweiser in St. Louis, but not in Chicago. For the 1956-57 season Falstaff President Joe Griesedieck thought some more publicity for the Falstaff Chicago team might help. "We're going to fly the Chicago Falstaffs to St. Louis each week and compete against the Buds," Griesedieck announced. "That way, we'll get publicity in both cities, plus some copy around the nation."

It didn't work. Falstaff failed to preempt Budweiser on the lanes or on the market. Still, Falstaff decided to keep its team in St. Louis, and under captain Buzz Fazio the St. Louis Falstaffs found some success. Fazio signed up some excellent bowlers: Nagy, Welu (a former Bud), and Harry Smith (a former Stroh). Falstaff took the national title

Above: *Under captain Buzz Fazio (foreground), who succeeded
Buddy Bomar, the St. Louis Falstaffs won both the ABC five-man title
and the BPAA team title in 1958. Standing, left to right: Steve
Nagy, Harry Smith, Billy Welu, Woody Hulsey, and Carl Richard.*
Opposite left: *In 1960, Sylvia Wene won the All-Star for the second
time and became the first woman to bowl a perfect game in the tournament.*
Opposite middle: *The big payoff—Milton Berle smothered Therman Gibson
after Gibson won the $75,000 grand prize on* Jackpot Bowling, New
Year's Day, 1961. Opposite right: *Though he died young, Nagy
established himself as one of the all-time greats in his brief career.*

from the Reserve Beers in 1957, after trailing by 552 pins at the end of the first half of the battle in Chicago. That year, too, the Falstaffs sizzled their way through the ABC tournament, earning the team championship and setting an all-time record in the all-events with a 9,608. They took the team title again in 1960 and 1963, and were the ABC Classic Division winners in 1964.

A final note on the heyday of the big teams. The matches between the brewery-sponsored classic league teams from different cities became, in effect, contests between those cities. Bomar explains, "We had matches all over, mostly against St. Louis, Detroit, Cleveland, Philadelphia, and New York. Teams represented sponsors, but they also represented cities. When we had a match against another city, we'd put the hottest bowlers in our lineup, regardless of which teams they bowled for back home. These matches were all home and home, usually for a thousand dollars. People also made lots of side bets, and if we were meeting Detroit, the pot would get up to fifty thousand."

Here were nothing less than professional major league teams—shifting all-star squads playing pot games, it was true, but no less popular for it. Bowling, with its individual superstars and marvelous teams, seemed to have conquered the sports public as both an individual and team game.

Above: *LaVerne Carter, the first wife of Don Carter, was a top-flight bowler in her own right.* Right:
Harry Smith belied those who called bowling a sedentary sport. Opposite: *In winning the 1962 All-Star, Shirley Garms sought—and evidently received—a little extra help.*

Boom Turns to Bust

To casual observers it seemed as if the game had never been healthier. There seemed to be hardly a street corner or shopping mall without lanes. Professional tours had begun, and there was word of a national bowling league that would formalize the professional team competition for men.

Insiders, however, detected some alarming signs. In 1957, the BPAA commissioned Ernst & Ernst, a New York management and accounting firm, to conduct a nationwide survey to be the basis for an "operating-ratio report." This survey discovered that the average bowling establishment made a profit of only 7.8 percent in 1956. The BPAA commented, "This startling disclosure was in sharp contrast to the rosy 25 to 30 percent being preached as gospel by so many builders and promoters of bowling ventures." In October 1959, another report by Ernst & Ernst found that the average net return for bowling houses in 1958 had plummeted to 2.4 percent. This survey also revealed that 26 percent of the establishments lost between 0.2 and 26.5 percent, and that another 14.5 percent earned only between 0.1 and 1.0 percent. It had become obvious that there were simply too many bowling centers.

By 1962, the helter-skelter expansion yielded the inevitable result. A devastating bust toppled hundreds of centers and cast a pall over the game. Milt Rudo, now Brunswick's vice-president/group executive of recreation, recounts the decline and fall.

"In the late fifties we started getting complaints from proprietors about overbuilding," said Rudo, then vice-president of marketing for bowling. "They said they weren't doing enough business, yet many kept expanding. In the summer of '62, proprietors began defaulting on payments for lanes and automatic pinsetters. Originally, our policy had been

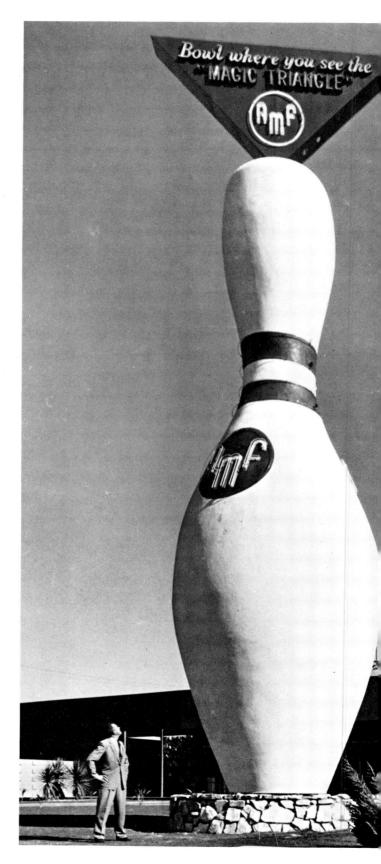

twenty-five percent down and five years to pay. In '62, as the situation got worse, we dropped this to five percent down and up to ten years to pay. But defaults and requests for contract extensions kept coming in. Jack Hanigan [then the president of Brunswick] doubted whether we should continue to sell. In the spring of '64, Hanigan decided there should be no reduction in prices and that the twenty-five percent down payment would be required. The collapse got worse [then], but Hanigan's move was wise because it kept those who didn't have proper financing from becoming involved. The bust was rough on us, and there were times we thought we'd go bankrupt."

Here are Brunswick's figures for repossessions during the height of the bust:

Year	Pinsetters	Lanes
1962	1,462	994
1963	3,354	2,595
1964	4,592	3,739
1965	5,996	5,276
1966	3,658	3,101
TOTALS	19,062	15,705

Tom Meade of AMF, now the chief executive officer of the company's bowling products group, says, "The sudden popularity of bowling in the fifties and sixties had made it the 'in' thing to do. It became a fad. Unfortunately, proprietors forgot some hard-learned lessons and didn't take care of the new people, so they left the game. The proprietors didn't see to it that those new bowlers were properly trained so they would stop throwing gutter balls and they would perform better and enjoy the game more. Another reason for the bust was the intense competition between manufacturers, primarily between Brunswick and us. A lot of investors were allowed into the game who didn't know anything about the bowling business and were not

By the late fifties, bowling loomed larger than ever over the American recreational landscape and, in this case, just the landscape. It was about to come tumbling down.

interested in its management. They didn't know how to secure the dedicated bowlers and how to help the new ones. Many came in on a financial shoestring. We all learned from our mistakes, but the lessons were painful."

To survive the hard times, Brunswick borrowed more than $250 million. The company endured, and by 1969, its repossessions had fallen to 783 pinsetters and 688 lanes. According to the most reliable estimates, some thirty thousand lanes and fifteen hundred centers closed during the bust.

Meanwhile, the top levels of the game experienced similar traumas. To cut costs the BPAA dropped its national doubles and team championships in 1967. Most of the best squads from the big-team era disbanded, the victims of spiraling costs and the new Professional Bowlers Association (PBA). The two biggest events in the sport were discontinued: the Chicago Proprietors' World's Invitational in 1965 and the BPAA's All-Star in 1970, both victims of the excessive costs of the large arenas in which they were held—arenas no longer filled with fans.

Marion Ladewig once summed up the attitude of most bowlers when she said, "Months before the All-Star I begin getting ready for it. There is nothing quite like it." Certainly not the new U.S. Open, an event on both the men's and women's professional tours that was supposed to replace the All-Star. The new Open stimulated none of the old fervor. The demise of the All-Star and the World's signaled the loss of what top-flight bowling is still trying to regain: the stature of a major sport.

Why this sudden plunge in the success of a pro game that had been flourishing? One of bowling's colossal failures, the National Bowling League, explained much of the problem.

In November 1960, NBL Commissioner Richard C. Charles said, "Don Carter hasn't signed with us yet, but before long he won't be able to afford to stay out. Inside two years we will have players in the one hundred thousand dollar bracket. After our World Series, all league bowlers will be eligible for the greatest tournament the sport has ever had—an eight-day championship in Madison Square Garden with two hundred and fifty thousand dollars in prizes, one hundred thousand dollars to the individual winner."

It was reported that the New York entry, the Gothams, would play on dazzling new $3-million

lanes "suspended in mid-air in Grand Central Terminal." A lucrative television contract for the league was said to be imminent. Supremely confident NBL executives hinted lightheartedly that they worried most about whether they should use their profits to pay off the national debt or to buy Europe and add it to the league.

In the end, which came virtually at the beginning, New York's entry did not play in the proposed marvel in Grand Central. Instead, the team wound up in Totowa, New Jersey, and was renamed the Gladiators. There was a World Series, but no eight-day, $250,000 championship event afterward. And there was no TV contract, which doomed the league.

No one, it seems, had seriously considered whether bowling could successfully adopt the format of a team sport. Perhaps the success of the big teams had lulled investors into the false assumption that a few intercity rivalries could be ex-

Some of the new centers were palatial (opposite top) and the new interiors more trim and functional than ever (opposite bottom). Unfortunately, the public backing wasn't quite there. Below: The biggest bust was the National Bowling League, in everything but public support a major league.

panded into a national league and, most important of all, packaged for a mass television audience.

In the unprecedented expansion of big-league sports at the time, bowling eagerly claimed its slice of pie in the sky, not realizing that what worked for some would not necessarily work for all. Football emerged from the war years to be embraced by television, for which the game was ideally suited. Baseball had more trouble adjusting. And bowling, in its new team format at least, bombed.

The NBL had its share of a new league's typical problems, including the absence of at least two big names—Carter and Weber—and an unrealistically long and concentrated schedule. But it also had, at least at the start, enthusiastic backers who were willing to spend generously (more than $20 million) for all the extras that would give the league a big-time image. It didn't work though, because, in the final analysis, bowling wasn't designed for it.

With the automatic pinspotter, bowling had be-

gun a period of overbuilding it could not sustain. With the NBL, the game indiscriminately followed other sports into a venture ill-suited for the television exposure any major league sport has to have. In the beginning, when television was new, audiences marveled at anything on it, particularly sports. Before long, though, every sport had not only to present itself but to sell itself. The sixties brought home these painful truths. Bowling learned that to recoup some of the eminence it had known in the pre- and postwar years, it would have to find a format of its own that could exploit the myriad possibilities of television. Fortunately, by this time a media maven, soon to become one of the most powerful figures in the sport, had begun to solve the television riddle. Eddie Elias and his Professional Bowlers Association tour were about to bring pro bowling into the electronic age.

Bowling Is Back

Like many wonderful ideas that seem exceptional in hindsight, a professional bowlers' tour seemed a lot less exalted when it was only an idea. As early as 1946 such proposals were made, yet nothing came of them. In 1958, when Akron lawyer-sportscaster Eddie Elias broached the idea again, the pros hardly overwhelmed him with their response.

At the BPAA national doubles in Mountainside, New Jersey, Elias asked some of the best bowlers to meet with him in his second-floor motel room. Six came. Before they heard what he had to offer, the bowlers were growing restless. The meeting was getting out of hand when 24-year-old Carmen Salvino, already a respected figure among bowlers, intervened. "I picked up a soda bottle and pounded it on the desk," Salvino says. "I told the guys, 'Hey, this man is trying to help us. Let's at least give him the courtesy of listening.'"

"Carmen saved the day," Elias admits. "After I spoke to the men a few more minutes, they wanted to know, 'Why are you trying to organize a tour?' I told them, 'Because you deserve to have true professional status and because I think I can make some money for myself.'"

"His honesty won us over," Salvino says simply.

Later that year, at the ABC Masters in Syracuse, New York, a larger group convened to consider the matter. Elias told them, "I'm not going to shower you with promises I can't keep, but I will give you a tournament circuit, a group insurance plan, television shows, and the opportunity to make a living at bowling." The date was May 24, 1958. Some seventy-five bowlers attended the meeting, in a hotel banquet room. Before the session ended, 33 agreed to risk $50 each to found the Professional Bowlers Association.

"We met again about a month later at Twenty

Don Johnson missed a perfect game (and a $10,000 bonus) in the finale of the 1970 Firestone by one ornery 10-pin, but Johnson's loss was bowling's gain. Millions watched the thrilling finish on television, as bowling proved it could rate with any sport in the battle for the television buck.

Grand Alleys in St. Louis," Elias recalled. "This time we met in the beer room in the basement and everybody sat on beer cases while I read the constitution I had drawn up. When I was done, Nagy hugged me. Then I knew we were in."

Three tournaments were held the next year, with Lou ("Wrong Foot") Campi winning the $2,500 top prize in the opener, the $16,500 Empire State, in Albany, New York. (Campi's nickname stemmed from his unorthodox delivery, in which he wound up on his right foot, just as he had always done while playing boccie.) Dick Weber won the other two events that year. Seven tournaments were held in 1960, two won by Carter.

As the emerging dominant member of the PBA tour at the time, Dick Weber rates special mention not only for his extraordinary success but his style, which signified an important change in bowling. Slightly built (5 feet 10 inches, 120 pounds), Weber nevertheless threw a powerful, sharply hooking ball in his early years. All the great ones did, in the tradition established when lanes were coated with shellac, a soft finish. Shellac allowed only powerfully thrown balls to hook; it slowed down others so much that it stripped them of their hooking power. In the fifties, a new, harder finish, lacquer, replaced shellac. Dressed with oil for protection, lacquer had an effect on the ball similar to that of shellac. But as proprietors sought to entice women to the lanes, they began to oil the lacquered lanes less than all the way down to the pins. Keeping the lanes oilless near the pins accentuated the hook of the ball there, just enough to assist weaker bowlers.

For the strong bowler, however, this shift in lane conditioning proved disastrous. The big curve balls and hooks of the past, dependent on evenly conditioned lanes from the head of the lane to the pindeck, now broke wildly out of control at the end. Bowlers such as Carmen Salvino found their games virtually ruined.

Weber adapted beautifully to the new conditions. He developed a modestly hooking ball, and he mastered the delicate art of adjusting it to the ever-shifting drying patterns of the oil dressing. As bowlers followed the lead of stars like Weber, the game gradually changed from one of power to one of finesse.

With the collapse of the NBL, the PBA lost its only serious competition for talent. As Elias lined up tournament sponsors and landed a television contract, the pros, once so reluctant, now flocked to him.

He ruled firmly over his bowlers. When he learned that some of them were grousing about lane conditions at a California tournament, Elias jetted out to confront them.

"I split the bowlers into three groups and saw each separately," Elias said. "When I walked in, you could have heard a pin drop. If you couldn't have heard a pin drop, I would have walked right out. They didn't talk to me. They *listened*. I said, 'I know you've got complaints and probably I agree with them. But think it over. Is this the time—in the middle of a tournament—to make a big *thing*? Think what you can lose.' And I let them think. 'Bowl now, complain later,' I told them. When I finished, they actually applauded."

The PBA grew impressively: 32 tournaments in 1962 (including a winter schedule carried on ABC-TV); a $1-million prize fund in 1963; a $100,000 event, the first Firestone Tournament of Champions in 1965; the first $50,000 individual yearly earnings in 1966—Wayne Zahn's $54,720 and Dick Weber's $50,605. Meanwhile, Elias kept his bowlers happily occupied in their spare time, making money on the television bowling shows. During the sixties, PBAers won $780,640 in cash, plus other prizes, on "Jackpot Bowling" and "Make That Spare."

In 1970, the Firestone Tournament produced one of bowling's most thrilling moments, which, thanks again to the television network, bowling fans across the country witnessed. In the title match both Don Johnson and Dick Ritger started with six strikes. Then Ritger left the 4-pin. Johnson did not leave anything and, after locking up the championship, he needed just one more strike for a perfect game, which would win for him a $10,000 bonus. His last shot zipped into the pocket perfectly and the pins scattered. But somehow the 10-pin remained standing. Incredulous, Johnson fell facedown on the approach and clenched his fists. The first to assist him to his feet was Ritger, who had lost the highest scoring match ever seen on national television, 299-268.

The seventies produced a superstar in the bespectacled left-hander from Tacoma, Washington, Earl Anthony. Within less than a decade after joining the tour full time, in 1969, Anthony ranked as one of the finest bowlers of all time. Weber said

94

Left: *Lawyer, promoter, TV-attuned Eddie Elias made pro bowling a success with his pro bowlers tour, founded in 1959 with the support of* (above, *left to right*): *Frank Carter, Pat Patterson, Don Carter, Steve Nagy, and Red Elkins.*

bluntly, "Earl has the greatest changes of speed of any bowler of any era." Anthony became the only man to be Bowler of the Year three times in a row and the only one to lead the PBA in both earnings and average three consecutive years (1973-75). In 1975, his earnings crossed the $100,000 threshold. His seven tour wins in 1975 set still another record. And in 1976, he brought his total PBA triumphs to 26, surpassing the previous leaders, Johnson and Weber, who had 25 each.

The PBA's television ratings made it apparent that pro bowling could command a mass audience. It came as something of a surprise, though, when game-show bowling on the most amateurish level did equally well. Beginning in 1968, "Bowling for Dollars" brought to television contestants who sometimes had difficulty keeping the ball out of the gutter, much less throwing the two strikes that won the jackpot, an average of one thousand dollars. Confounding the experts and critics, the show branched out to more than twenty markets, and spawned such offshoots as "Duckpins for Dollars" and "Candlepins for Cash."

Perhaps the explanation was really very simple: people watched because they bowled, most of the time, pretty much like the all-too-fallible contestants.

A generation after "going bowling" had be-

In the seventies, Earl Anthony (opposite), *succeeded Dick Weber* (below) *as the best of the pros, surpassing Weber in lifetime victories and money-winnings on the PBA tour. While Anthony led the men, a new woman star emerged in Betty Morris (left), who in 1977 won her second Bowler of the Year.*

come as common a phrase as "going to the movies," bowling continued to flourish. In addition to the ever-growing number of serious bowlers, tens of millions more Americans played the game casually. It made an ideal recreation—cheap, easy to learn, convenient, accessible. There were rarely long waits, as on the golf course or tennis courts, and it was a year-round sport. Men and women could enjoy it together.

But to all these reasons, one must add a certain intangible—call it tradition, or custom. For at least a generation American children had been growing up with bowling. Bowling establishments had become as much a part of the American landscape as fast-food outlets. The game had become a cultural habit—something America had always enjoyed and, through all the social shifts of the sixties and seventies, saw no reason to abandon. More than a sport, bowling had become part of almost every American's heritage.

Surely the biggest bowling news of the decade has been not the stars but the extraordinary resurgence of the recreational game. Not only are more people than ever before bowling, often in such classy centers as Don Carter's Kendall Lanes (opposite), but more are watching other, strictly amateur bowlers on television. The ratings of Bowling for Dollars *(above), whose jackpot winners go home elated but rarely rich, have astounded the experts, who assumed game shows had to offer big money to be successful. The message is clear enough: it's the game, not just the show biz, that people enjoy.*

3. A Home on the Road
The PBA Tour

On August 22, 1970, in Waukegan, Illinois, Benjamin Franklin ("Butch") Gearhart of Ft. Lauderdale, Florida, married Susi Baker of Houston, Texas, with Justice of the Peace Paul Kilkelly presiding. Because the groom happened to be working that day, the ceremony was held where it wouldn't take him away from his business. And so the couple got married in a local bowling center. They marched under crossed ten pins held by Larry Lichstein and Bob Alstott and exchanged vows between lanes 19 and 20. Veteran bowling writer Joe Richards gave the bride away.

Butch Gearhart is a pro bowler. It's not that his work is so demanding that it doesn't allow him a day off to get married. It's just that a pro bowler gets very absorbed in what he is doing. He quits home for so long to pursue bowling that the pro tour becomes a new home—to him and those two hundred or so other unrooted sportsmen who fancy that they can make a living at bowling.

They have all met the requirements for membership in the Professional Bowlers Association (PBA): a 190 average for at least two years, character references from a PBA member and others, and $150 membership dues. They each invest $155 in entry fees for every tournament they enter. Most never break even. Their fancy averages from back home have a way of slipping on the tour. In any case there isn't enough prize money to support more than a few dozen bowlers. The few top ones win a modest fortune in endorsements beyond their prize money, plus a following among bowling fans. The rest stay on only if they can afford to lose or because they can't admit failure.

The PBA tour is not always a happy place to be. However, despite the hardships, and in a way because of them, it's a warm, very human community. There is little room for animosity among men who are trying to overcome odds as large as the ones the tour presents. The pro bowlers are competitors, of course, but there is a remarkable camaraderie among them, as if they value just *being* pro bowlers as much or more than the success they might achieve as such. As foster homes go, the pro bowling tour is one that a person can grow very attached to. Someone might even choose to get married there.

The PBA's annual schedule consists of three major tours. The winter season starts in the first week of January, lasts 17 weeks, and climaxes with the richest bauble of the year, the $150,000 Firestone Tournament of Champions, in April. In early June the summer tour begins its 10- to 13-week grind. Some of the bowlers are joined during the summer by their wives and children, adding a certain festivity to this junket. During the summer it is not uncommon to see children playing with toys and dolls at the back of a bowling center while their fathers try to make a living on the lanes. Last, there is the fall tour, which runs from mid-October until December. Approximately forty regional events held throughout the year sweeten the financial pot.

Not all the pros on the circuit are full-timers. Many compete for only a few weeks. Some choose events on the winter tour because there is more money to be won then. Others pick summer tournaments because a lot of regulars skip them. And still others limit themselves to the events that are close to home. One such local entrant, Steve Nowicki of Rochester, New York, entered the PBA National Championship in Rochester, in 1972. It was a hectic week for him: he had a full-time job as an accountant for Monroe Lithograph and an obligation to bowl for the Harding Supply team during the midweek session of the Western New York Classic League. Somehow, he managed to fulfill all his commitments and finish twenty-seventh in the Nationals, good for $555.

For all but the local entrants, a tournament week starts and ends with travel. Other professional athletes complain about the rigors of flying from city to city throughout their seasons. Almost all bowlers *drive* from site to site, sometimes covering more than a thousand miles between destinations. There are no traveling secretaries to hand out tickets, make hotel reservations, and arrange connections. Trips aren't always made alone, but they are made informally. "If ya wanna go with us, be in the lobby in fifteen minutes," is usually the substance of a group's travel plans.

Flat tires, radiator boilovers, and cracked hoses are considered just so many routine occupational hazards. In Wickiup, New Mexico, a bowler's car once simply blew up. En route to Denver from the Showboat Invitational in Las Vegas one Saturday night in 1976, Jack Andolina ran aground in Rifle, Colorado (population: 2,150), when his car's water pump went "on the fritz." He had to be in

Overleaf: *Lanky Dave Davis stretches even longer and leaner under the eye of a special effects lens.*

Top: *King of the road Larry Lichstein poses with his traveling headquarters, where he both lives (left) and works (above). As director of player services, Lichstein serves as a clubhouse man* extraordinaire *for the PBA bowlers.*

Denver the next day for a pretournament qualifier, in which contestants compete not for cash but for the few remaining berths in the PBA tournament to follow, in this case the Denver Open. (Pretournament qualifiers first became part of the PBA tour in 1976, when six were held.) So Andolina left his car in Rifle to be repaired and rode a bus for seven hours to Denver. There he bowled well enough to qualify, took another seven-hour bus trip back to Rifle to pick up his repaired car, and finally drove back to Denver for the start of the tournament. At last his road weariness caught up with him. He failed to cash at the Open, and his shuttling went for nothing.

Carmen Salvino tells a story of the bowler's ultimate travel travail. In 1968, Salvino had entered a PBA event in Caracas, Venezuela, where a revolution was brewing. On the way to the lanes one day, Salvino's cab was halted by armed men. They searched the cab and found what they were convinced were bombs. Tommy guns were pointed at Salvino, and he was ordered to stand against a wall. Amid much jabbering and gesticulating, the veteran bowler finally managed to determine that the "bombs" were nothing more than bowling balls in which the finger holes had not been drilled. Fortunately, he managed to convince the armed men that bowling balls don't explode.

"Leapin' Lizard? D'ya hear me, Leapin' Lizard? This is Montana Masher. You and me, we're gonna shoot it out tonight, and when I'm done with you, they'll pick you outa the gutter."

Nothing sinister there, just some citizen's band radio banter between pros on the road. "Montana Masher" is the code name of Rick Perry from Columbia Falls, Montana, and his shootout opponent on the lanes is Larry ("Leapin' Lizard") Laub of San Francisco. Other CBers in the bowlers' caravan have been Bill ("Texas Yanker") McCorkle, Mike ("Wheely Wagon") Berlin, Mickey ("Cookie Monster") Higham, Dennis ("Tennessee Warhorse") Lane, Bob ("Omega Man") Singleton, and Jim ("Kegler One") Stefanich.

Laub was one of the first pros to invest in a home on wheels. In 1974, he lost his motor home and everything in it when a leak developed in the propane gas system, which triggered an explosion and fire that completely destroyed the vehicle. Laub was bowling at the time; he walked out of the

bowling center to find his home gone. Undaunted, he bought another. During almost any tournament these days, motor homes can be spotted outside the bowling center, clustered together to hook up to a central electrical supply.

One of the first drivers to appear at each stop is Larry Lichstein, whose title of director of player services barely hints at the diversity of his labors. He supplies the pros with everything from newly drilled balls to Rolaids, for all of which he earns tips and fees apart from his PBA salary. Lichstein assumed the job after quitting the pro tour (he was Rookie of the Year in 1969) because he "couldn't put up with the mental strain." At 5 feet 11 inches, 145 pounds, Lichstein looks less than durable. When his game was deteriorating on the tour and a doctor told him he was becoming musclebound on his left (bowling) side, Lichstein quipped, "I didn't know I had any muscles."

Lichstein travels the circuit in a refurbished Greyhound bus. "When I bought the bus, for ten thousand dollars, it was seventeen years old and had a million two hundred thousand miles on it," he says. "Then I went to work on it."

He installed water tanks, a bathroom with shower, and a kitchen that has a four-burner gas range, oven, sink, and refrigerator. There is more yet: stereo, central air conditioning, two beds, and just about all the comforts of home, which for Lichstein is Suffield, Connecticut.

In the rear of the bus, Lichstein has set up a small pro shop, complete with ball-drilling apparatus. Growing numbers of bowlers are coming to rely on Lichstein for ball drilling. As he moves around the bowling center, they often seek him out to hand him slips of paper on which they have written specifications for new balls that they want him to drill for them. Some don't even bother to list the specifications, confident that they'll do well with whatever he produces for them. After Dave Davis won the 1974 Firestone Tournament of Champions using a ball that Lichstein had drilled only minutes before, Davis remarked, "Larry really knows bowling balls. And he knows lanes, whether they will hook early or late. An hour before the TV show in Milwaukee [at the Miller High Life Open in 1975], he punched out a new ball for a pair of lanes we hadn't used in the tournament. Larry told me that he thought I could score from the inside. I tried about fifteen balls from there and smashed the

No one has ever suggested of Mark Roth that he makes it look easy. One of the hardest throwers on the tour, Roth bowls with ferocious intensity.

Other athletes have a clubhouse in which to change; bowlers use a "paddock," a cramped, cluttered dressing room even when there's no one in it (below). When the bowlers arrive (opposite), the best strategy seems to be to stand still. Right: Four bowlers cope with the ordeal of close quarters changing while one relaxes from it.

pocket fourteen times. Then I moved back outside and goofed around so the other lefties [Earl Anthony and Johnny Petraglia] wouldn't find my secret strike line." Davis won that tournament, his first victory in five years.

Veteran great Dick Weber says of Lichstein, "He can put weight any place you want in a ball. Larry can watch you bowl and give you the help you need. He's uncanny."

In large storage bins in his bus Lichstein keeps 12-foot-tall metal leader boards, about 125 bowling balls belonging to the pros, and another 75 that he himself owns. Most bowlers have a dozen or so bowling shirts to wear during tournaments. To spare themselves the bother of toting these around and having them cleaned, they pay Lichstein a nominal fee to do it. So Larry has made room in his bus for some one thousand shirts. About nine o'clock every Monday morning he delivers a surprise for a local cleaner—two hundred shirts to be dry cleaned.

Back at the bowling center, Lichstein and his helpers lug their goods into the bowlers' clubhouse. This is usually the game room or a converted, crib-filled nursery, where in nontournament weeks bowling parents leave their youngsters. In these quarters Lichstein sets up tables on which to weigh each ball to be used. Then the serial number of every ball is jotted down on a bowler's file card and the hardness of each ball is measured on a durometer. In 1973, this durometer check became all-im-

107

portant, after Don McCune discovered that soaking balls in a chemical compound called toleune softens the shell, giving the ball better traction on the lanes, which means higher scores. McCune, who had won only two PBA titles, suddenly took six in 1973, led all the money-winners with total earnings of $69,000, and was named Bowler of the Year. The PBA and American Bowling Congress (ABC) had to intervene, outlawing the soaker and establishing minimum hardness ratings for bowling balls.

As further preparation, Lichstein and his helpers hoist several steamer trunks laden with sundries onto various tables. He supplies an electric sander, drills, sandpaper, and beveling knives for repairing bowling balls. Other goodies include: lighter fluid, cigars, gum, mints, shoe brushes and polishes, hair sprays, deodorants, shoelaces, bowling gloves, and medical supplies such as Band-Aids, aspirin, nasal sprays, throat lozenges, cough drops, indigestion remedies, and the court plaster bowlers apply to their tender fingers.

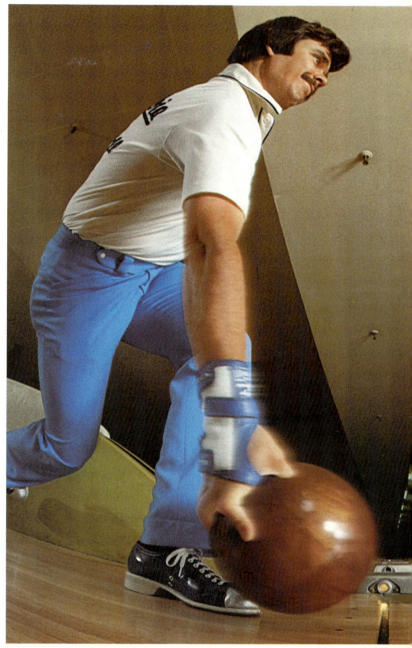

Opposite: *Multiple-image effect catches the perfect balance of Jim Stefanich.* Above: *Paul Colwell at the explosion point seems to have almost more than he can handle.* Left: *Tommy Hudson's release.*

Sore, swollen, bleeding thumbs torment many bowlers. In their attempts to find relief, these bowlers have been known to soak ailing digits in brine or other solutions, or even to stick them in holes gouged in potatoes. The most notable of today's Terrible Thumbs is Mark Roth of Staten Island, New York, who from 1974 through 1977 was the second leading money winner on the PBA tour with $260,881. Roth has been forced to withdraw from tournaments, and has sometimes had to sit out entire competitions, because of a throbbing thumb. His difficulties come from the forceful crank he gives the ball upon release, the same motion that gives his ball extra power. Like other thumb sufferers, he could cure the ailment by changing his delivery. He and most others like him prefer to put up with the pain, rather than risk tampering with their style. So they go on torturing their thumbs, hoping to keep the discomfort to a minimum with the plasterlike substance and other salves that Lichstein provides.

By the time he has finished setting up shop, Lichstein has begun the transformation of the clubhouse from a spacious empty room into the most cluttered and crammed dressing room in sports. In addition to all of Lichstein's equipment, the room houses wall-to-wall bowling bags and racks of shirts along the walls. For bowlers, there are no carpeted clubhouses with neatly stenciled nameplates set above spacious personal lockers. Nor are

Paddock pastimes—top: *catching up on the home folks;* above: *grooming under duress;* left: *drying court plaster.* Opposite: *occupational hazard.*

111

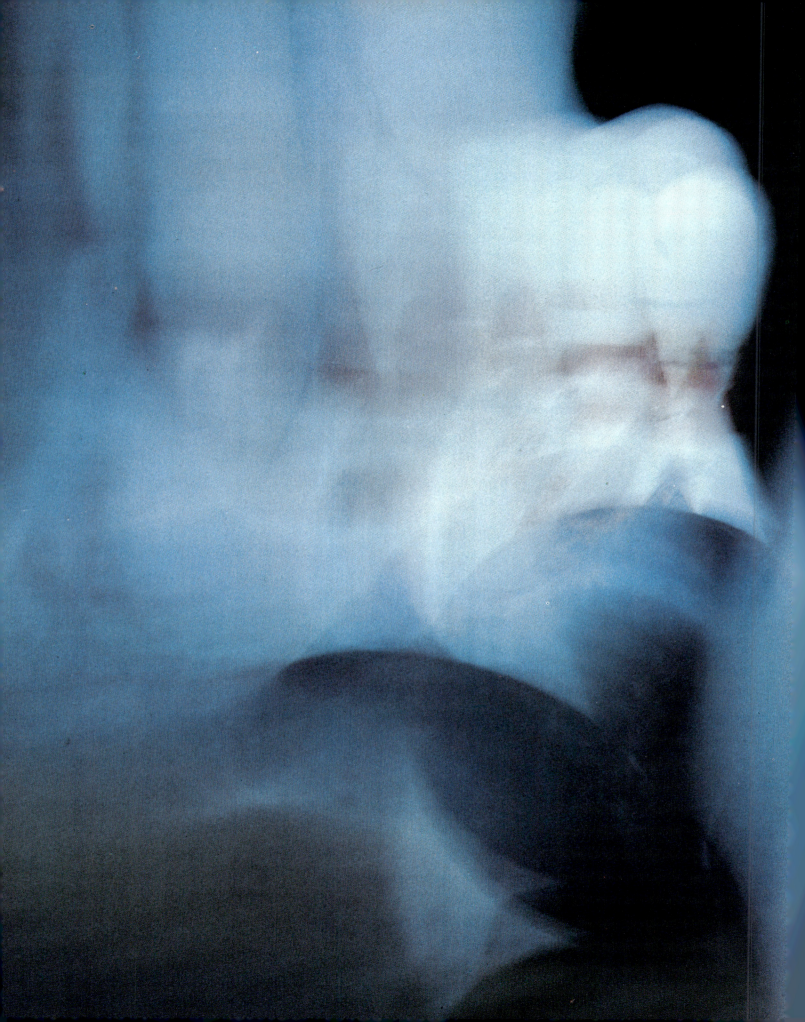

there tiled showers, attendants, trainers, doctors, or free postgame meals in the clubhouse. Horses have had better accommodations than those pro bowlers are often subjected to, which may be why the clubhouse has been dubbed "the paddock."

Experienced pros can move about the paddock as nimbly as mountain goats negotiating a tiny ledge. Others sustain stubbed toes, bruised hips, even jabs in the abdomen from quickly drawn billiard cues. Crowded though it invariably is, the paddock often contains a pool table, somehow wedged among all the bowling paraphernalia. A bowler once tried to claim a little space for himself by appropriating the pool table as his personal couch. He stretched out on it, folded his hands be-

Milwaukee, underwrites the operational costs of the tournament in return for the proceeds. For a bowling proprietor or commercial organization, running a PBA tournament is more prestigious than profitable. But unlike the proprietor or commercial group, the charitable organization can elicit tax-free donations from the community. Added to the take from ticket sales, concessions, and the invariably lucrative pro-am event, such donations can make the operation of a bowling tournament a successful fundraiser. Through running PBA tournaments in New Orleans from 1974 to 1977, the Lions there earned more than sixty thousand dollars for their camp for crippled children.

Pro-am tournaments have become so popular

hind his head, and closed his eyes, only to awaken a short time later to find that his comrades had stuck a cueball between his lips, had racked up the other 15 balls at his feet, and were firing away.

Most PBA events are financed and organized along similar lines. Usually a commercial sponsor puts up the prize money for a tournament. A bowling center proprietor provides the facilities and—in conjunction with a local organization—covers the operational costs, including personnel such as mechanics, scorers, and desk-counter attendants. Occasionally, a civic or charitable organization, such as the Sertoma clubs in Houston, the Lions clubs in New Orleans, or the Multiple Sclerosis chapter in

that some of them now run for as long as two or three days, almost as long as the PBA tournament they precede. At Dallas in 1975, 1,260 adult amateurs took part in the pro-am. Children swelled the pro-am entries to as many as 1,700. Some tournaments have special programs for youngsters, complete with gifts and trophy-studded banquets. Andy Varipapa's Stars of the Future tournaments on Long Island, New York, have been among the most successful of these pro-am youth events.

Amateurs can buy a spot in the pro-am or they can earn their way in. Either way the house gets its entrance fee, usually $50 per person (except when youngsters are admitted free). To buy a spot, an entrant simply pays his $50. To qualify for a spot, he

Overleaf: *Even the biggest smoothy on the tour, Earl Anthony, glares with concentration as he bowls.* Above: *"Ladies and gentlemen: the world's finest bowlers." Each shift begins with such a parade.* Opposite: *Fans back their man in a cluster.*

CONNER
SMITH
WOOLET
MEYERS
AVG. 204
SER. 759
279 WERBECK
ROTH
RITGER
47
49
50

Opposite: *Gary Dickinson glows when he bowls.* Above: *Steve Jones won the first tournament of his career in 1977, then lost the touch when his index finger became strained.* Above right: *Carmen Salvino is a senior citizen on the tour these days.* Right: *Tommy Hudson struck it rich in 1977.*

gets together with some friends and chips in his share of the cost of an entry. Then the group holds a rolloff, the costs of which are also shared, and the winner gets the coveted pro-am spot as his prize.

In pro-am competition each amateur bowls in a group consisting of as many as seven other amateurs and one professional, who anchors the group. He signs autographs for his partners, offers bowling advice when asked, and does his best to help his partners win some money. (The adult winners often receive as much as $1,500; the pros themselves are ineligible for prizes.) After each person in the group has bowled a game, the pro switches to another group. This procedure is repeated until every group has bowled three games, each one with a different pro. The score for each amateur consists of his handicap added to his three-game pinfall and the scores of the three pros for the games they rolled with the amateur's group.

After the pro-am is completed, the tournament begins, with the field divided into two equal groups —A and B squads. Each of these squads is further divided into four-man units for every pair of lanes. Thus, the entire field can be no greater than two men per lane per squad, or four times the number of lanes in the house.

The two squads begin the tournament by bowling in three separate shifts each during the first day and a half. One squad usually begins at 9:30 A.M. and 4:30 P.M. of the opening day and at noon of the next day; the other squad might start at noon and 7:30 P.M. of the first day and at 9:30 the next morning. (To keep things strictly equal, squads alternate starting times each week.) Each squad is carefully balanced with an equal number of champions, so a fan can have his choice of watching name bowlers no matter when he shows up.

Usually, each pro bowls six games per shift. After each game he switches to another pair of lanes with the other three members of his four-man crew. This musical-chairs aspect of the qualifying rounds makes it necessary to have foursomes that bowl at more or less the same pace, lest tie-ups develop.

The man in charge of this traffic management, and virtually everything else at a tournament, is **PBA National Tournament Director Harry Golden.** If the slender Lichstein is something of a guardian angel to the pros, Golden is the father confessor. It is only a slight exaggeration to suggest that the pros live by the Golden Rules—that potpourri of

Opposite top: *Lineup boards show names of all bowlers in the tournament, divided into A and B squads.* Opposite middle: *Leader board shows scores in total pinfall above 200 per game.* Opposite bottom *and* left: *From the looks of Dennis Lane and his scorer, she's a schoolteacher and he just flunked.*

edicts, instructions, explanations, and just plain friendly advice that Golden is forever dispensing. Surely one of the most competent officials in all of sports, Golden has presided over more than five hundred PBA tournaments since assuming his job as tournament director, in 1961.

"For a couple of years I ran a bowling center in El Paso, Texas," he says. "I also bowled on the tour for a while in '60 and '61. And I promoted the El Paso Open in '61. After it was over, I sent a six-page critique to Eddie Elias [founder and president of the PBA] about what I felt the PBA had to do. It so happened that Elias had recently signed the first contract with ABC-TV for coverage of the winter tour. That, plus the awareness that he had the makings of a summer tour, gave Eddie the realization that he had a year-round project. Elias then knew he needed someone to be a full-time tournament director—not just a local person or a couple of people from his office staff. I got the job and I've been out here ever since."

Except for an ever-present bottle of Maalox and a hairline that has been reduced to little more than a ring around the scalp, Golden seems hardly to have been taxed by his long stint at the hub of the PBA whirl. With dapper dress, a mellow voice, and a confident stride, he cultivates an aura of being in perfect control of a tournament at all times. As he talks about himself and his job, he gives some indication of the commotion that surrounds but never seems to faze him in his work. He seems to have an explanation for everything.

"All the personnel at a tournament are my responsibility—the mechanics, scorers, control-counter people," he begins. "When I give my instructions to the scorers before a tournament, I tell them they're liable to hear cuss words when a bowler has a bad shot. But I ask them to be tolerant.... We don't allow bowlers to get out of hand, though, and there are fines for a variety of things, including kicking a ball-return rack.

"I'm also the umpire-in-chief on foul or pinfall disputes. If anything happens *in front* of a bowler—a pin falling out of the automatic pinsetter, for example—then I might rule in his favor. If it occurs *behind* him—a Coke bottle being dropped on a terrazo floor or a baby screaming just as a bowler shoots—there is, unfortunately, nothing I can do about that. Now that I've said that, though, I remember a case where a metal nameplate of one

Opposite: *Larry Laub cultivates the golden boy look.* Above: *After a shift, particularly a discouraging one, the young hopefuls are not quite as spritely carrying their balls around. Ron Woolet is the weary-looking one here.*

bowler fell off the leader board and clanged to the floor just as Don Helling was bowling. That was a tough question for me because the leader board was not in back or in front of the bowlers. It was off to the side. I determined that the noise had bothered Helling, so he was able to take his shot over, and he got a strike. In 1976 in Denver, someone opened a side door at the lanes just as Mickey Higham was shooting a seven-pin for a spare. The sun glared right on the lane in front of Mickey and he missed the pin by a foot and a half. I talked to other bowlers who saw what happened and then I made my ruling: Higham could take the shot over. He did and he made it. At one center there were lots of crickets. Just as Sammy Baca started his approach in the tenth frame of a big game in which he needed a strike to win, he stepped on a cricket. You could *hear* the crunch. After the lane was cleaned off, Sammy started all over. This time there was no trouble and he got his strike."

Before each shift, Golden or an assistant arrives in the clubhouse to conduct roll call, a proforma check that every member of the squad is present. For a moment the amiable chaos of the clubhouse subsides. Golden stands unruffled, almost serene, among the crowd of bowlers and clutter of equipment. The bowlers stop to listen for their names and any announcements. Then, the ritual completed, the hubbub grows again. Bowlers check for mail in the shoe box that serves as their post box. The men pluck clean shirts off the racks and tend to their hair with brushes, combs, or hair dryers. (Mirrors, for some reason, are in chronically short supply.) Zzztt, zzztt—spritzes of spray deodorant are applied. Finally, it's time to go, and the men troop out for their shift.

After the claustrophobic paddock, the lanes are only a slight improvement. Once a tournament begins, the bowling center is shrouded in cigar and cigarette smoke so thick that the air conditioning system cannot dispense it, and a smoglike haze often hangs over the lanes. Bowling establishments were not built for large crowds, but most are able to seat at least a thousand fans on bleachers installed for the tournament. Empty seats are usually hard to find.

The very proximity of the fans to the bowlers makes for an intimacy between spectator and performer rarely found in other sports. The fans take snapshots and movies at the lanes. When the bowlers switch lanes, more than a few of the fans follow them, moving through the bleachers so that they can sit behind their favorites again and again. They cheer and clap, and many keep score. These mavens can spout bowlers' records as readily as baseball nuts can recite pros' batting averages and ERAs.

A folksy fanfare greets the pros as they arrive to start the tournament. There is taped music and the unchanging introduction (also taped): "The finest bowlers in the world." Colorful pennants, bearing the names of past champions, festoon the lanes.

As the men shuffle to their assigned lanes, they seem a motley bunch, carrying their bowling balls pressed against their stomachs, resting atop their shoulders, dangling from their fingertips, or even (once in a great while) spinning on their forefingers, Globetrotter style. Then the men are introduced to the crowd by Golden, take a few practice shots, and begin rolling in earnest.

While they bowl, an overhead projector displays their scoresheets to the fans in back. Next to the name of the contestant, the scoresheet displays a black or red number, which indicates the bowler's overall score in much the same way a golf scoreboard lists a golfer's score as under, over, or even par. However, in this bowling equivalent of golf's par system, it's good to be over par, bad to be under. The equivalent of par is 200 pins per game. The figure next to the bowler's name shows the difference (plus or minus—black or red) between his accumulated score and the number of games he has rolled, multiplied by 200. If, for example, after 10 games he has an overall score of 1,900, then the number will be 100 in red (minus). If his overall score is 2,100 after 10 games, the screen will show a black (plus) 100 next to his name. At the end of each shift, newly computed red or black figures for each bowler are registered on large lineup boards, which carry the names of every bowler on each squad. The names of tournament winners are printed in black, nonwinners' in red. What with black numbers on the projectors for good scores and black lettering on the lineup board for past champions, pro bowlers like nothing better than to see their names blackened.

Except for the television finals of a tournament, the pro bowlers move from one pair of lanes to another. Consequently, widely varying lane conditions are the rule, not the exception. Back home,

When not bowling—and even on tour they're usually not—pro bowlers never quite escape the performer-on-the-road lifestyle. Top: *Dave Heller does some housekeeping (mobile-home variety);* above: *Dennis Swayda peddles Indian jewelry and sex appeal;* left: *back in the paddock again.*

123

the bowlers could spend all night rolling on the same set of lanes, priding themselves on being able to "read" those lanes and to rack up big scores. On the tour they no sooner adjust to one pair of lanes than they must move to another, which to their dismay turns out to be vastly different. A pro finds himself continually altering his speed, his angle of delivery, and his rhythm in an attempt to navigate the ever-changing lanes. The inside line that worked so well on lanes 13 and 14 may be disastrous on 17 and 18. A 235 score on one pair of lanes can plummet 50, 80, or even 100 pins on the adjacent pair.

"I like to watch new guys come on tour," says PBA veteran Gus Lampo of Endicott, New York.

"They've all had success at home, but out here a lot of them get crushed when they can't cash in the tournaments. So many of them just can't cut the conditions. They're used to rolling on the same two lanes all night and running up big scores. Out here they find they have to shift from one set of lanes to another after each game, and they can't adjust to how different the conditions are from one lane to the next and from one pair to another. One guy had a two thirty-five average back home. He came on tour and *never* cashed in three years of trying off and on."

Call it guesswork or intuition—probably much of it is—but the winning pros have an uncanny knack for solving the riddle of the lanes. At the

Brunswick World Open in Chicago a few years ago, Earl Anthony was bowling poorly the first day. Afterward he decided that a ball he had at home was better suited for the lane conditions. He recalls, "I keep the serial numbers of those balls with me, so I looked up the one I wanted, called my wife, Marylou, back home in Tacoma, and told her to get that ball out of the attic and try to get it on a plane that night. She did. I bowled the next day with that ball, which turned out to be just right for me, and I wound up winning twenty-five hundred dollars for finishing third. That made the eight-dollar airfreight charge a good investment."

Two weeks before each tournament PBA officials inspect the lanes, bowling on all of them and establishing specifications for the care of each before and during the tournament. Theoretically, the lane conditions can be made very nearly uniform by varying the application of oil, with which every lane is dressed. The more heavily used parts get more oil, the other parts less. Unfortunately, it's not that easy. Each lane is different in the pattern and rate its oil dries up, so each lane has to be treated individually. And as soon as play begins, the differences in the lanes begin to reappear. Many pro bowlers have observed that lane conditions change not only from one tournament to the next but from one day to the next, one hour to the next.

Then, too, there is the righty-lefty problem. As most bowlers know, the left side of any given lane

The day of the TV finals the house bustles everywhere but on the lanes. Above left: *mechanic's view of practice—Dick Weber up.* Top right: *Chris Schenkel miked up and in place.* Above right: *Schenkel confers with producer Bob Goodrich, center, and PBA liaison Frank Esposito, left.*

invariably gets less wear than the right, because most bowlers are right-handed. The righties wear a small, almost imperceptible groove—called a "track"—in the right side of a lane. Even when the lanes are dressed with a fresh coat of oil over the finish on the wood, this track remains, because it is actually a rut in the finish. To rid a lane of its track, a bowling center proprietor has to have the finish removed, through a process called "screening." This takes place before most tournaments, but the track soon begins to build up again as play progresses.

If one knows where it is and how to use it, a track can be an advantage—a line to the pocket. However, it takes time to find and take advantage of a track, and continually switching lanes, the pros have little time to become familiar with them. The right-handers must cope as best they can with the track and the other problems of greater wear on their side of the lanes, whereas the lefties bowl on relatively even surfaces.

The righty-lefty problem has provoked loud arguments and accusations. In one game at the 1971 Firestone Tournament of Champions, Dick Weber and Nelson Burton, Jr., two right-handers, rolled backup balls from the left side of their lanes to protest what they considered lane conditions that greatly favored lefties. (Weber rolled a 201. Burton, who threw a few balls left-handed, had the lowest score of his PBA career, 109.)

Despite all the attention it receives, lane maintenance persists as a problem on the PBA tour and is likely to remain one at least until the new, artificial lane surfaces are installed, making conditioning a less delicate skill. The man who until recently had the thankless chore of grooming the lanes, former Lane Maintenance Supervisor Len Nicholson, seemed resigned to never being able to please all the bowlers. The 6-foot 3-inch, 270-pound Nicholson once speculated, "I think I got my job mainly because of my size."

Six games and some three hours after leaving the paddock, the squad returns there, many of the men exasperated by diabolical lane conditions, Gibraltar-like 10-pins, and (though these are rarely mentioned) their own failings. Some of the bowling balls that were handled so carefully a few hours earlier are now deliberately and disgustedly dropped on the floor. Those men who have bowled well seldom congratulate themselves in the paddock. They limit their conversation to subdued clinical discussions of the conditions, out of respect for those who did poorly. A quick hair combing, zzztt, zzztt, a fresh shirt, and the bowlers are off for a meal and a chance to rest.

Perhaps the greatest challenge to a pro bowler is to use his spare time constructively. If he can relax, putting the day's successes or disappointments behind him and clearing his mind for the next day's round, he may be doing more for his game than any adjustment he could make on the lanes could. In any individual sport a player has to guard against becoming obsessed with his problems. Nobody improves his game by sitting alone in his hotel room feeling sorry for himself; yet faced with boredom, loneliness, and discouragement, most pros have gone into seclusion at one time or another.

Some bowlers spend as little time as they can at the lanes, showing up just in time for roll call and departing as soon as they have finished their last game. Others linger in the bowling center restaurant, sipping coffee, eating, and table-hopping —story-swapping and gossiping. Or they get together over a drink at the bar. Still others fiddle with their equipment at a workbench in the paddock, which can be as solitary during a shift as it is crowded before and after one.

More and more pros are investing their spare time in exercise. Johnny Petraglia practices karate; Dick Ritger jogs a few miles a day. Many others swim in the motel pools, do calisthenics in their rooms, or visit the local YMCA to play basketball, lift weights, or play handball. Frisbee on motel lawns has become a popular pastime, though more in the nature of a time killer than a training aid.

Time-killing has become almost creative among pro bowlers. Once while waiting in the laundromat for clothes to be washed and dried, Davis, Petraglia, Skee Forensky, and Dave Soutar bought a set of plastic horseshoes and pitched them around the laundromat, prompting startled looks from other patrons as they sidestepped skittering nonringers. Matt Surina once bought a Tinkertoy set and amused himself by erecting bizarre structures and contraptions with it. Curt Schmidt is said to have developed his addiction to pinball machines so keenly that he can sense one within a two-mile radius of the bowling center.

Tournament Director Harry Golden orchestrates the television show as he has the entire tournament. Top: *prepping the audience;* bottom: *briefing the mechanics.*

Occasionally, the diversions for the bowlers take the form of group activities planned in advance—a corn and pig roast in Davenport, Iowa; a golf tournament in Fresno, California [usually won by Jim Stefanich]; a day at Great Adventure Amusement Park in Jackson, New Jersey; and the PBA no-fair-sitting-on-the-puck ice hockey contest, held each year at the King Louie Open in Kansas City, Missouri, where a rink is part of the sports complex that includes the bowling center.

Occasionally, the leisure-time activities take on a theatrical aura. A tall blond man walks into a bowling center, places two attaché cases on top of the control counter, glances over his shoulder, and snaps open the cases, revealing rows of rings, necklaces, bracelets, and other jewelry. A swarthy Italian drifts around the lanes, confiding to certain bowlers, "Prayer meeting tonight at ten in Room Twenty-two." The men he speaks to acknowledge him with nothing more than a nod. Obviously, he is passing along a coded message. Another dark-haired, middle-aged man is sitting at the luncheonette counter. He casually places a tea bag in his mouth and closes his lips, leaving the string and label dangling across his chin. What's going on around here?

Well, the blond is 6-foot 4-inch, 215-pound Dennis Swayda of Phoenix, Arizona. No, none of his jewelry has been stolen. Swayda buys most of it from the Zuñi and Navajo Indians and sells it while on tour to supplement his bowling income.

The sinister-looking messenger is Teata Semiz of River Edge, New Jersey. Yes, his "prayer-meeting" message is coded. At ten o'clock in Room Twenty-two he and some fellow pros will convene for an evening of poker and another card game, *panguingue*, better known as "pan." Pan is complicated and esoteric: it is played with eight decks of cards from which the eights, nines, and tens have been removed. It is also frustrating: one player once ate some cards. Nevertheless, pan is the most popular card game on the tour. Some marathon games make Curt Schmidt's sessions at the pinball machine seem like pit stops. A pro once joined a game of pan at midnight and announced, "I'll play till noon," only to be trumped by another, who responded, "I'll play till the twenty-second."

The man at the lunch counter is Carmen Salvino. A startled waitress stares apprehensively at the string and label hanging from his lips. Blandly,

Salvino points to his mouth and asks, "Could you pour in some hot water, please?"

Back to business. At the end of the second day, when 18 games (that is, the three 6-game blocks for each squad) have been completed, the field is pared to the two dozen highest scorers. Each remaining bowler rolls another 23 games—one against each of the other 23 contestants. The winner of each head-to-head contest has a bonus of 30 pins added to his total score. If there is a tie, each bowler gains a 15-point bonus. The total scores of the 24 are tabulated, and each man rolls a twenty-fourth game in a "position-round" match to determine the final ranking of the 24. The number-one scorer after the twenty-third game goes against number two, and so on down the line through number 23 versus number 24. Thus, after the position round, the bowlers have rolled a total of 42 games—18 in the first two days, 24 in the remainder of the tournament.

If there is a televised finale, and most tournaments now have one, the top five bowlers after the position-round match qualify. The American Broadcasting Company, which carries the winter tour, sends a 35-man crew to work late Friday night, after the position round, to prepare for the Saturday afternoon telecast. The crew works through the night, stringing lights, erecting camera stands, positioning monitors, laying cables, and hooking up assorted electrical gear. PBA Hall of Famer Frank Esposito coordinates the operation. Among other things, he meets with the five finalists and coaches them for the Saturday performance. His instructions range from general common sense ("Stay loose and do what comes naturally") to picayune particulars ("Please coordinate your socks with the rest of your outfit"). He reminds the bowlers not to talk to their opponents during the match. "Years ago we got a lot of flack from viewers because Tom Hennessey patted Don Carter after a shot," he tells the five contestants. "You don't want to give the impression you are not trying to win. And let's face it, you are not *really* glad the other guy made a nice shot."

As some twenty-million viewers know, the television tournament consists of a four-match progressive elimination. In the first match, the number-five finisher in the position round faces the number-four finisher. The winner goes against the

Bowling in the television finals bears little resemblance to the game in the qualifying rounds. For one thing, you're suddenly all alone (top). Pete Couture, Wayne Zahn, and Bill Spigner (above left to right) *show their cool under the lights.*

Right: *Mike Durbin in dreamland at the 1977 Firestone Tournament of Champions.* Below: *Paul Colwell coaxes the 8-pin on his last ball in a bid for a perfect game at the 1977 Quaker State Open. (It fell for him.)*

number-three man. The winner of that match progresses to the semifinals against the number-two man, and the winner there meets the number-one man for the championship.

The TV finals contrast dramatically with the rest of the tournament. After days of bowling amid the rumbling of other matches on other lanes, the finalists perform before a hushed audience, on a brightly lit stage of just two lanes. All the others lie silent, except two spare lanes on which the bowler for the next match warms up, careful to take his practice shots when none of the competing bowlers is up. The crowd, packed around the two center lanes, erupts in hopeful shouts as soon as the ball hits the alley. If the ball strikes, it sets loose a wave of cheering; if not, a chorus of groans. Primed for television by Golden, the crowd good-humoredly hams it up on cue, the model studio audience.

For 16 years, ABC has been televising the *Pro Bowlers Tour*, the second longest running of all sports series. Only college football has lasted longer. "I get more feedback from these shows than from anything I've done except the Munich Olympics," says Chris Schenkel, the longtime announcer for the series. "It's amazing the number of people—a lot of them doctors and other well-to-do individuals—who watch bowling." Surveys reveal that the audience is almost identical to that for late-night talk shows: upper middle class, from larger households, in metropolitan areas, and from relatively well-educated families.

The ratings are solid. Pro bowling has steadily held its own in the weekend TV sports blitz. During one weekend in 1975, for example, the viewer ratings results read: NIT basketball—9, NCAA basketball tournament—31, bowling—30. Later that year, two weekends of head-to-head competition between pro basketball, major league baseball, and bowling showed basketball with a combined rating of 43, baseball with 47, and bowling with 49. And when the bowlers went against golf, the third round of the Masters Tournament, no less, they won 25 to 21½. Furthermore, it has been found that an average of three people per TV set watch bowling, compared to an average of only a little more than one per set for golf.

That's the good news. The bad news is that pro bowling blinks off in the nation's sports consciousness as soon as the TV lights go out. Television brings the game to 20 million viewers, but the press starves them of any sports fan's meat—the oddities, controversies, and personalities. Often, the papers don't even carry the scores. A reader of the New York *Times* can find English football scores and dog show reports more readily than bowling results. Supposedly lower brow papers publish no more. Among sports editors, pro bowling seems to rate slightly above pro wrestling—more than a sleazy exhibition but not really a sporting event.

No one would dispute that pro bowling is a legitimate contest. But apparently many consider the pro bowler little more of an athlete than a pool player or card sharp. The physical stress of the game is minimal, and there appears to be an underlying assumption among people who don't understand bowling that it is too mechanical and repetitious to be much of a challenge. There is not enough action, say the detractors, and then they somehow conclude that there is also not enough skill. These charges are at best misleading, at worst downright untrue. No one refutes them better than athletes who have come to pro bowling from other sports.

"Bowling is the hardest sport I have ever tried, and I've played quite a few, including football, baseball, basketball, and golf," says Bill Sudakis, a former major league baseball player. "*Every* shot counts so much in bowling, and there are terrible mental and physical strains that I was not aware of when I was just bowling for fun. It's hard to believe how difficult this sport is." The pro tour quickly convinced Sudakis. He entered 10 tournaments and earned no money in any of them.

Larry Seiple, a punter for the Miami Dolphins, tried his hand at pro bowling for a brief period in 1976. "I thought I had been under all the pressure an athlete could endure," he reflected afterward. "But to have to make one shot and to have no teammates to help you, that turned out to be tougher than anything I had ever experienced. . . . I couldn't believe I'd ever get that nervous. I've played football in the Super Bowl and in front of eighty thousand and a hundred thousand people, but the twenty-five hundred fans at the lanes during [my first] tournament . . . unnerved me far more than any crowd ever did.

"Like a lot of other people, I've watched pro bowlers for years on TV and in person. I guess we all tend to say, 'That's easy,' [but that's] because the pros make it look like it is. Then you get out there to throw the ball, and it doesn't come off your

thumb. After a while, you get so flustered you don't know which way to turn or how to make your feet go. . . . I can't understand how pro bowlers do it, constantly knowing they've *got* to make a shot so they can feed their families. . . . That's *pressure*."

Clearly, the professional bowler's coordination, precise timing, and, above all, ability to withstand mental strain make his sport as demanding in its way as are sports that are physically far more punishing. As Sudakis and Seiple found out, the game on the professional level only looks easy. Some years ago, a machine was designed that was supposed to be able to roll a bowling ball to produce a strike every time. Much engineering know-how went into the construction of that machine. When it was finished, it was matched against some pro bowlers. The bowlers won this man-versus-ma-

chine competition, because they, unlike the machine, could detect subtle changes in lane conditions and adjust their shots accordingly.

Contrary to popular opinion, almost all the top-flight bowlers are continual students of their sport. At the head of the class is Carmen Salvino, age 44, one of the 33 pros who threw in with Eddie Elias to form the **PBA** in 1958 and one of two left who is still a regular on the tour. He earned his stature the hard way, after new, harder lane surfaces ruined his hook—one of the most sweeping and powerful in history—and his game collapsed.

Salvino's salvation turned out to be a mechanical engineer who had the outlandish idea that bowling could be reduced to a mathematical equation. Skeptical, not to say downright opposed at first, Salvino slowly accepted the idea and eventu-

ally effected a comeback that demonstrated as never before that pro bowling is, or at least can be, a thinking man's game.

The miracle worker was Henry Lahr, a former bowling companion of Salvino's. Late in 1969, Lahr proposed to his friend that they work together. Lahr brainpicked Salvino for all he knew about bowling, the two men examining bowling for eight, ten, twelve hours a day, not always amicably. "We reevaluated the game in terms of pure physics and geometrics," Lahr says. "For six months I taught Carmy the basics of physics and engineering so we could communicate. We invented a language, a combination of terms for laypeople and engineers. I taught him some of Archimedes' principles, the basics of logic, and even vector analysis, which is a postgraduate course.

"I developed theories, but for a long time they all failed. Then we began to make progress. There is an equation in physics defining the motion of a pendulum. But there are two kinds of pendulums: controlled and free swinging. It has always been said that a bowler *must have a free swing*. But I proved mathematically that to bowl properly you need a *controlled* swing. Two other important things that we found concerned heat transfer and conservation of energy. After we worked these into mathematical equations, the problem was to get Carmy to bowl like a machine.

"If a three-hundred hitter slumps, it's usually because he doesn't know what he's looking for. He's proven he has the talent to hit, but that's not enough. He also needs knowledge. What can you learn from practice if you don't know what you're doing? Carmy had to learn the value of knowledge —how to think, how to solve problems. I taught him the uselessness of being negative. I said, 'Tell me *one* way that being negative will help.' He couldn't. This may sound easy, but it's not when a man is in a deeply negative state."

By the summer of 1971 it was evident that Salvino's game had been rebuilt. Not unexpectedly, he had also grown in stature as a man. "It's incredible what Hank Lahr did for me," Salvino said. "He gave a year and a half of his life to help me. We're like Damon and Pythias. Hank organized my mind and my game, and he made me a human equation. I'm a lucky man."

In 1973 came their reward. After five winless years, Salvino won the Lincoln-Mercury Open championship in New Orleans. He took four more titles in the next four years, boosting his total to sixteen. In 1974, he was named a charter member of the PBA Hall of Fame.

So much for the charge that the game is repetitious and mechanical. It *is* repetitious and mechanical, but that doesn't make it easy, any more than golf is easy because the golf swing is repetitious and mechanical. And as for a lack of action in pro bowling, is a ball hit with a golf club any more gripping than a ball rolled down an alley? It is hard to escape the conclusion that sportswriters and sports editors don't really know bowling and for that reason fail to cover it adequately.

Naturally, the pros resent the second-class status of their sport. It robs them not only of recognition but of money, for if bowling had the glamour (that is, the publicity) of golf or tennis, then surely the prize money would rise. As it is, the purses are a small fraction of those in golf and tennis. In 1976, the PBA offered a total of $2.75 million in prize money, compared to the Professional Golfers' Association's $9.157 million.

"I won six tournaments in 1969 and earned sixty-four thousand dollars for the year," recalls Billy Hardwick, by far the top money winner among bowlers that year. "If I had won the golf tournaments that were being played those same weeks, I figured I would have made a hundred eighty-five thousand. And that's not counting seconds, thirds, fourths, and other finishes that year. The bowling tour is a good place to starve."

Of course, $64,000 is hardly a starvation wage, but in bowling even the top money winners are not far removed from those who barely break even. The division of the prize money is such that only one-third of the contestants finish in the money. Depending on the size of the field, that comes out to between forty and ninety money winners. Those at or near the bottom of that select list earn too little to cover their expenses, and even those in the middle are in jeopardy of running into the red. It takes a bare minimum of $350 per week for a pro to earn his keep on the tour. Only about fifty bowlers average that much or more in earnings.

"In golf you can make it if you finish between here and here," says Golden, stretching his hands two feet apart to convey golf's relatively generous prize structure. "In bowling you must finish between here and here." Golden's hands move to six inches apart. "I respect any bowler who has the courage to come out here and try to make a living, and I wish him all the best of luck. He'll need it. . . . Making a living on the bowling tour is the hardest way to make it in sports."

Given the scarcity of prize money, the pro tour becomes an ordeal for the competitors. Every pro pits his confidence, in himself and his game, against the inescapable economic odds that tell him he won't make it. Yet the very absence of big money and publicity has its advantages. Excluded, however unfairly, from the riches of the great American spectator sports' bonanza, pro bowlers have remained human beings, not the mass-media, bigger-than-life celebrities that athletes in other sports have often become. Pro bowlers are about the most unassuming, accommodating profes-

Mod men Ernie Schlegel (opposite) *and Barry Asher* (above) *tend to disconcert the TV people and delight everybody else with their glad rags.*

sional athletes there are. Bob Goodrich, who produces many of the ABC bowling telecasts, testifies, "I have been involved with every major sport, and I find professional bowlers to be the nicest, most cooperative, down-to-earth athletes."

As a group, pro bowlers form one of professional sports' more closely knit communities. Players in other sports who have belonged to the same team can be less supportive of one another than pro bowlers who are competing against each other. Facing the same stern challenges together, with a shared sense of only themselves to fall back on if they fail, pro bowlers have more of a spirit of empathy than rivalry for one another. "These guys eat together, travel together, share rooms, tell each other their problems, and then they try to beat each other's brains out on the lanes," marvels former Director of Player Services Clyde Scott. "The amazing thing is that they don't hold grudges. I guess that after being out here for a while they realize they're all in this thing together and they respect each other because of that."

Everyone on the tour has received help from another pro. Such assistance extends beyond the common courtesies of reminding someone of his starting time or picking up and returning such items as wallets, sweaters, or eyeglasses, which the bowlers habitually leave around bowling centers. Denny Turner of Stockton, California, who joined the tour in 1974, remarked shortly after joining, "The people out here have been great. . . . I needed help with my game a couple days ago. Scotty [Clyde Scott] kept saying, 'I don't have time to help you. I don't have time to help you.' But then he came out to the lanes to watch my shots and to talk with me. The guys are nice, too. Like today, I came in after a bad opening day and Tim Albin tapped me on the knee and said hello. Or a Carmen Salvino will come up and tap me on the shoulder. Little things. But the thing is they make you feel pretty good, and when you get to the point where you believe the guys think you're a good person, well, that's a nice feeling."

"I remember being really broke when I was at a tournament and having a meal with Ray Bluth," Billy Hardwick remembers of his first, less-than-successful year on the tour. "He ordered a steak and I ordered a hamburger. When the food came he said, 'Oh, I forgot that today's Friday. I can't eat meat on Friday.' Bluth gave me his steak; it was his

135

way of making sure I ate a decent meal for a change. So many of the big guys were really fantastic to me."

In 1965, at age 18, Johnny Petraglia headed out on the tour, having financed the venture by hustling his way through a string of one-night stands at numerous New England lanes and pocketing $1,200 by cleaning up in pot games and on side bets. PBA life looked easy at first. Petraglia won $300 in his first tournament, then hit for a quick $1,750 in two others. Soon, however, overconfidence and the rigors of the tour caught up with him. When lane conditions were right for his big curve, Petraglia rolled well, averaging 225 for six tournaments. At other times, however, his average dropped to 175—a typically erratic rookie.

"You could see he had the talent," says Sammy Baca, a touring pro in those days. "He just needed guidance. I'm always watching guys bowl. But you never shove your knowledge on another player. Bobby Jacks was a young bowler then, too, and he asked me for help. I worked with him and he won the next tournament, in Brockton, Massachusetts. Johnny noticed and asked me to help him. I pointed out a few things to him. He tried them and said they didn't work. I told him he hadn't tried long enough—he was impatient. Then Jacks won his *second* tournament in a row. Next morning there's a knock on my door. It's Johnny. 'I think I'm as good as Jacks,' he says. Now he wanted help."

Baca drilled a new ball for Petraglia. Eighteen of the rookie's first twenty shots with that ball went into the gutter. This time, though, Petraglia stuck to it. "He was walking ahead of his swing and had to bring his arm around his body to make up for it," Baca remembers. "We worked on that and his rhythm, and the next week, in Fort Smith, Arkansas, Johnny won for the first time. He appreciated my help and sent me two hundred dollars. He's that kind of a guy—a real gentleman."

After a stint in Vietnam, during which his weight fell from 170 pounds to 145, Petraglia returned to the tour. He did not win a penny the first four weeks back. Again, another pro helped out, this time Skee Foremsky, a fellow southpaw. "Sammy Baca had changed my whole game and helped me a lot and Skee put the finishing touches on it," Petraglia says. "He drilled different balls for me for different lane conditions. And he taught me to relax and bowl *my* way." Petraglia has now won

nine more titles, five in 1971, when he was Bowler of the Year.

Somehow, such success stories outshine the more numerous ones of desperation, delusion, and ultimate defeat. "I've seen so many guys who want to make it *so bad* out here," says Roy Buckley, a veteran pro bowler from Columbus, Ohio, no doubt vividly remembering his own lean early days on the tour. He and other pros speak of "out there" as if the tour were a lonely outpost in a combat zone. They see many casualties. "I've seen guys try all sorts of ways to save a few dollars so they can keep going for just one more week," Buckley continues, "because every one of them feels he is on the verge of making it big. I've seen guys walk a couple of miles each day between the lanes and the cheap little rooms where they're staying, just so they wouldn't have to spend the money for transportation. And I've seen them stop along the way to their rooms to buy a can of tuna for dinner. It makes me ache when I watch them struggle like that."

"There was one guy who came on the tour and was so bad it was hard to believe," says Clyde Scott. "At one tournament he was worse than ever. It hurt to watch him. A couple of us tried to talk him into dropping out of the tournament and said we'd arrange so he wouldn't have to pay a fine for getting out. He said, no, he'd stick it out because he had a two hundred eight average back home and he knew he'd do better as soon as he got the hang of things out here. It was sad and funny to watch him. . . . And you had to feel sorry for him because he was so bad that guys were betting on whether he would make single-pin spares. He missed so many that if you'd bet a beer that he'd miss you would've been drunk during every round the poor guy bowled."

What makes someone risk this psychological and/or financial devastation? A good person to ask is Dick Berger—a man who during six years on the tour never won a tournament and seldom cashed. Not until an aching back forced him to the sidelines in 1976 did he finally quit the tour. Discussing his reasons for staying with it despite his perpetual failure, Berger and his smiling wife, Mary, touched all the traditional reasons. They cheerfully admitted being captivated by the chance to make their favorite recreation their occupation, even if they didn't make any money at it. A successful plumbing contractor, Berger could afford not to

Marshall Holman comes from the-bigger-they-are the-harder-they-fall school. This one, at the 1977 Burger King, fell big and beautiful, and not quite painlessly, it seems.

Closing scenes–top left: cue card in place for the *TV wrap-up; top right:* paddock remnants; *above: Lichstein (with helper)—first to arrive, last to leave.*

win on the tour. Even so, losing wasn't easy.

"The aggravation is terrible at times, and I really don't know why we're out here," Dick began.

"Yes, you do," responded Mary. "You love it out here."

"You're right; I do."

"Besides, you're too stupid to quit, and so am I. Everything we like most is out here on the tour—bowling and bowlers. And you know that someday you'll put it all together and your game will be better than ever."

"The best I ever did out here was eighth in Toledo in 1973. I had a shot at the TV finals, but Norm Meyers beat me, two forty-seven to two forty-six."

"Dick's happy out here," Mary said, starting to smile at her husband. "So if this is what he wants, this is where we'll stay."

Recounting their efforts to kick the tour habit, Dick concluded, "We dropped off the tour and bought a small bowling center that opened in June 1972. We thought of all the drawbacks of the tour—eating out all the time, planes, packing, five hundred dollars a week or more, and then we rushed right back out here again."

Most bowlers, like any other underpaid workers, lament the lack of money to be won. Unlike some others, though, they are dedicated to what they do. They confess that they enjoy their work, despite its problems, and they are proud of the camaraderie they share with their fellow pros. They are among that vanishing breed of athletes who are prepared to sacrifice, rather than demand, extravagant compensation for being the best in the world at what they do.

A few years ago, the tour bowlers had a wild victory party following a tournament in Fort Worth, Texas. All the celebrants wound up in the hotel pool, clothes and all. When the dunkings ended and the participants stood drying off at pool-side, somebody happened to notice one last remnant of the celebration at the bottom of the pool: the winner's first-place check.

Not to put too heavy an interpretation on that incident, it's fair to say that pro bowling has yet to take the plunge into the era of the almighty buck. Strictly from the standpoint of a fan who likes his athletes to be human beings, too, the game may be better off that way.

4. Still a Long Way, Baby

The Women Pros

In 1970, Dotty Fothergill of Slatersville, Rhode Island, applied for membership in the PBA and was turned down because of her sex. She then initiated a lawsuit against the PBA to force the organization to accept her application. The parties settled out of court, and Fothergill never tried again to become a PBA member.

Another woman star, Patty Costello, a lefty from Scranton, Pennsylvania, tried a more conciliatory approach. In 1976, she expressed considerable interest in competing on the PBA tour "if she was invited." She wasn't.

It should surprise no one that the male pros feel they have no room for women on their tour. For one thing the prize money there is already stretched too thin for most of them. What was significant about the experiences of Fothergill and Costello is not that they failed to crack the all-male barrier but that they tried at all. In a sport that women can play almost on a par with men, the women pros have for the most part failed to command equal pay for equal work.

"For a short burst, a good female bowler is very capable of beating a male bowler in a head-to-head match," explains Roger Blaemire, commissioner of the Professional Women's Bowling Association (PWBA). "Over the long run, the man will beat her because of his endurance and strength. In golf Judy Rankin couldn't beat Jack Nicklaus even in a short match. She would have to be given a handicap just to keep up. It's a different sport. Bowling is the first sport that really pits them equally against each other. In bowling one match, I don't know if Earl Anthony could beat Patty Costello."

It's a tantalizing question but, for the women bowlers who tried to compete on the men's tour, not the most relevant one. They were less interested in challenging the male stars than they were in just earning some more money. Women's pro bowling just didn't offer enough. "I wasn't trying to start any trouble," Fothergill explains. "I just wanted to bowl and there weren't enough women's tournaments around, so I felt I should give the men's tour a try, if possible."

Unlike women's tennis and golf, which have grown up quickly to match, and even pioneer, the rapidly rising status of women professional athletes, women's pro bowling is at best, just now beginning to break through. The agonizingly slow progress of the women's game remains one of the

The only time the women pros command purses equal to those of the men is when they bowl in tournaments with them (albeit separately). Opposite bottom (left to right): Mark Roth, Jay Robinson, AMF VP R. R. ("Woody") Woodruff, Betty Morris, and Edie Jo Neal at the 1977 AMF Grand Prix. Opposite top: Bucky Woy promised wonders for the women but on the whole didn't deliver. There were some bright spots, though, such as the first nationally televised PWBA event, when Woy posed with the top finishers (left to right): Judy Soutar, Loa Boxberger, Maureen Harris, Donna Mowad, and Cheryl Robinson. Top and bottom: The recent merger of the PWBA and the LPBA, headed by Roger Blaemire and Janet Buehler, respectively, may initiate an era of greater harmony for women's pro bowling. The new group is called the Women's Professional Bowlers Association.

Overleaf: *Betty Morris displays the beauty of a fine bowler's form, attainable as readily by women as by men.*

great conundrums of the ten-pin sport. After all, it was not long after the PBA was formed that the women pros got their start.

The PWBA was conceived in 1959 by Georgia E. Veatch, with an assist from Mary Bundrick. After drawing up a tentative constitution, Veatch wrote to outstanding female bowlers and proposed that they meet during the World's Invitational tournament that year. On December 2, 1959, in Chicago's Pick Congress Hotel, 23 women bowlers signed up as charter members of the PWBA. Nine months later, at North Miami's Pinerama Lanes, 100 women took part in the first PWBA tournament, several traveling all the way from California. The winner was Marion Ladewig, one of the established stars of the day.

The women were eager to bowl. What they did most, however, was wait. Four years after its founding, the PWBA was offering only four events for the year. Veatch explained, "We could conceivably sponsor more than four tournaments, but I don't want to chance it just yet. One failure could topple most of what we've built up." Not all PWBA members agreed with Veatch, and a faction within the organization began to press for her removal. Six years later, after nearly a decade of frustration, the insurgents prevailed. Veatch resigned on April 1, 1969. Mickey Finn, the loquacious manager of North Kansas City Bowl, replaced her as executive director.

When Finn took control, he confidently predicted that the women would at last attain prominence, with more tournaments and the start of television coverage, both of which he assured them were imminent. He lined up a $30,000 tournament in Las Vegas, the richest the women had ever had.

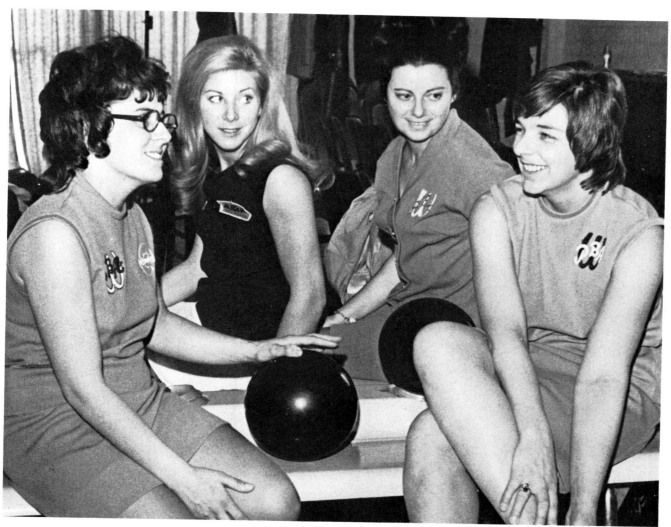

Opposite: *In the sixties all-time great Millie Martorella competed for prize money even less than that of today.* Above: *a quartet of southpaws around 1970—left to right: Fothergill, Sperber, Baker, and Costello.*

145

After two years, though, Finn admitted he could not oversee the tour and also work as a bowling center manager. He, too, faded away.

Into the breach stepped William ("Bucky") Woy, a rotund sports promoter from Akron, Ohio. Woy also promised big things for the still-floundering group. The women became quick believers and awarded Woy a 10-year contract. He gave himself the title of commissioner, moved PWBA headquarters to Akron, and billed the women as "the world's greatest and prettiest bowlers." More substantively, he produced the $55,000 Rick Case Honda Classic, the richest PWBA tournament up to that time, and then topped that with the $85,000 Brunswick Red Crown Classic, which gave the women their first national television exposure. He relentlessly pursued television executives and potential sponsors but generally encountered quiet resistance and indifference. On the strength of his early successes, the women expected big things ("He promised us a million-dollar tour," moaned Cheryl Robinson), only to be disappointed again and again. Finally, on December 29, 1974, disenchantment with Woy culminated in his removal.

Goodbye Bucky. Hello nobody. Anxious to take their time in finding a new leader, the bowlers themselves ran the tour for a short while. The PWBA headquarters was officially moved to Oklahoma City so that Toni Calvery could take charge of the operation. Other members also helped.

Finally, Ira Haynie was selected as the PWBA's new executive director. The group's headquarters shifted to Irving, Texas, where its new tournament director, Wyatt Slaughter, found some free office space. Haynie lived up to his reputation as a fine administrator, but he wasn't much of a promoter, and he did not stay long on the job.

On January 1, 1977, Roger Blaemire replaced Haynie. Blaemire had shown his promotional flair as a member of All-Sports Productions, a Chicago group that produces sports programs for television. Having witnessed through that firm the meteoric rise of the Ladies' Professional Golf Association (LPGA), Blaemire was optimistic that the PWBA could achieve similar success. Moving the PWBA headquarters back to its birthplace in Chicago, Blaemire vowed finally to bring the women out of the shadows. "Bowling might be a blue collar sport," he admitted, "but blue collar workers are buying as many Cadillacs as white collar people.

But the Cadillac folks won't tell you that."

Former Tournament Director Wyatt Slaughter, who left the PWBA to tend to his bowling centers in Texas, felt that Blaemire's marketing expertise would be just what the PWBA needed. "Until Roger came along, the PWBA was never sold right," he drawled. "And there was also so much change in leadership that before I came along the tournaments were never run professionally."

By this time, a new women's bowling group had sprung up. Janet Buehler, a businesswoman and lawyer from Canton, Ohio, formed the Ladies' Professional Bowlers' Association (LPBA) to fill the vacuum created after Woy left the PWBA. Buehler promised to bring "new opportunities to the professional lady bowler."

The opportunities were not many. The LPBA thought relatively big, seeking prize funds in the $25,000-to-$50,000 range, yet by the end of 1977 it had staged only six tournaments. In contrast, the PWBA staged about a dozen tournaments annually, though most of their prize funds range between only $10,000 and $25,000.

Were two tours better than one? It depended, of course, on whom you asked. One school of thought held that competing tours gave the women the best chance to raise their earnings: more tours = more tournaments = more money. "Let both groups run their tournaments," said Frank Coburn, whose wife, Doris, belonged to both the PWBA and the LPBA. "All it means is more money for [them]. In the end, the group with the best operation and the most money will survive anyway. After all, the same thing has happened to other sports. The World Football League collapsed because the NFL [National Football League] did a better job."

Others contended that women's bowling would never attract the outside support it so clearly needed until its internal affairs were in better order, which did not allow for the luxury of rival factions. Obviously, Blaemire belonged to this group. "We proposed a merger to the LPBA," he claimed. "When the talks broke down, we conducted our tournaments on an invitational basis, extending invitations only to girls who held just a PWBA membership."

And so the PWBA escalated the conflict between the organizations, obviously expecting most of the women to side with it and its more lucrative tour. The LPBA responded by going to court to keep

The Coburn family of Buffalo, New York, includes three women pros—mother Doris, and daughters Kathy and Cindy (right). Their manager is husband/father Frank.

membership in both organizations and participation in both tours open to all women. As the battle raged, some PWBA bowlers even agreed to boycott LPBA events.

Meanwhile, Blaemire rewarded his women by prying sponsorship commitments from three non-bowling corporations and contracting with the Mizlou television network to air five PWBA events in 1978. This swelled the PWBA prize money pot to $700,000 for the year, more than double what it had been when Blaemire took over. The PWBA seemed well on its way to producing a $1-million tour and winning its battle with the LPBA.

Suddenly, Woy re-emerged, claiming that the PWBA owed him money from his stormy stint as commissioner. He had made the claim before, but this time he was armed with an injunction, which enabled him to attach PWBA purses until his contract was satisfied. This situation prodded the

Above: *Judy Soutar, a veteran pro, won her first pro title in 1973, also the year of her first of two Bowler of the Year titles.* Left: *Virginia Norton rolled the PWBA's first 800 series.*

PWBA to resolve its difficulties with the LPBA, forming a new group beyond the reach of Woy. "With Woy making noises again," said Blaemire, "we felt it was time to make peace with Janet and her group and present a united front. We both made concessions, and now that Woy can't do anything with the new group, we feel we can move ahead."

This marriage of convenience dissolved the two competing organizations and formed a new one in their place, the Women's Professional Bowlers Association. The new group became a legal entity effective January 1, 1978, with Blaemire as commissioner and Buehler accepting an executive post (special events chairman). All members of PWBA and LPBA automatically became members of the new WPBA, making the new organization's membership about three hundred fifty bowlers.

Betty Morris (above) *and Patty Costello* (left) *battled it out for Bowler of the Year in 1977, with Morris eventually winning, her second such title.* Opposite: *Bev Ortner and the scorecard of her WIBC-record 818 series.*

151

To become professional bowlers, these women have averaged at least 175 in league play. Most have then advanced through higher competitive levels, such as sweepstakes tournaments sponsored by individual houses ("sweepers") and other local competitions. Many have developed their games in the semiprofessional women's bowling organizations that abound throughout the country: the Western Women Professional Bowlers on the West Coast, the Women's All-Star Association in the East, the Southwest Women's Masters, which headquarters in Texas, the Great Plains Association of the Midwest, and the Ladies' Tournament Bowlers group, headquartered in Ohio. (The PWBA also recently introduced its own regional network, which has already provided local competitions for some of its pros.)

To make the jump from regional to national bowling takes money, of course, which most of the women have to raise. Betty Morris, one of the premier figures in women's bowling today, staked herself to start-up money when she and her husband, Bob, sold their house in Ione, California. The house money was almost gone when she started winning, in 1974 (the year she first became Woman Bowler of the Year).

Cleveland's Debbie Vacco sold $100 shares of stock in herself to 30 investors. "They call themselves 'The Godfathers,'" she says of her patrons. "Mostly they're people around the bowling center who have seen me bowl and wanted to help me get started. Some of them even gave more than a hundred."

In addition to seed money, a woman pro, like her counterpart on the PBA tour, needs a competitive edge that sometimes borders on a compulsion to win. The women pros may be considerate and ladylike in appearance, but their competitive fires burn as brightly as do those of the men.

"I was shy, a real wallflower when I was in high school," remembers Morris. "Then I started bowling with my Dad. As I got better, it built up my confidence. Finally, I got the determination to be better than anybody else."

"You don't belong on tour unless you have a real need for your ego to be superior," contends Vesma Grinfelds, a winner of more than one event. "[You have to want] to be better than anybody else at some point, whether it be for one game, an entire tournament, or a whole year. If you don't feel that

Opposite top: *Paula (Sperber) Carter proves that pro bowling is one sport in which femininity and athletic prowess needn't clash.* Opposite bottom: *Cheryl Robinson agonizes quietly.* Left: *Pam Rutherford ready to celebrate.*

you have that desire to win, you don't belong on tour. I know I have that drive [though] I don't want to feel that it shows so much on the outside that I appear to be negative or rotten when I'm competing."

The women have patterned their tournaments after the PBA events. One major difference: instead of corporate sponsors, still rare for women's tournaments, the sponsors are likely to be the hosting proprietors, who run the tournaments as a promotion for their businesses. If the proprietor does a good job of promoting the tournament, it's a guaranteed boost for his bar and restaurant business as well as the other concessions he has at his center.

To host a women's event, the proprietor and his local sponsor, if any, put up a minimum of $10,000. This sum goes into the prize fund of the professional event, as do the accumulated entry fees of the competing pros (from $135 to $160 per bowler, depending on the event). The proprietor retains half the pro-am fees, the gate receipts, and whatever advertising revenue he accounts for by selling space in the PWBA's program book.

The pros usually come to town for four days. The first day is usually devoted to the pro-am, in which the local amateurs pay a fee to bowl with the pros and also compete for a small prize fund of their own. The pro competition starts the next day, with the pros rolling two qualifying blocks (six games each). On the third day, they complete their 18-game qualifying with a final 6-game block, and the field is then cut to the top 18 pros. These bowlers return later that day to start the match-play portion of the tournament. On the fourth day, they return for the completion of the match play, which consists of 18 games in all. If the tournament is televised, regionally or nationally, the top five bowlers return on the fifth day for the stepladder TV finals, run according to the format devised by the PBA for its tournaments.

The very paucity of women's tournaments makes them morely lively than the men's. Fans who have attended men's and women's tournaments are quick to comment on the difference in atmosphere between the two. For the men the succession of weekly tournaments quickly becomes a grind. For the women the few tournaments rate as special occasions, and there is a festive air about them. "Just being out here for a few days is like a vacation for lots of us," says one of the bowlers.

154

Opposite *and* left: *Donna Adamek and Chris Saunders play the waiting game with more hope than confidence.* Above: *Vesma Grinfelds assumes a striking pose.*

*Bowler of the Year in 1972 and 1976, Patty Costello
is the winningest woman pro bowler of all those active.
In 1977, she won her sixteenth pro title since 1971.*

As a rule they enjoy it to the hilt. After a tournament in Lafayette, Louisiana, for example, a number of the bowlers partied until 5:30 A.M., at which hour some decided it was time to head for breakfast—in New Orleans, about eighty miles down the road.

One Halloween night during a tournament in Mobile, Alabama, in 1969, the women marched out to bowl in costumes: ". . . caterpillars, pumpkins, Yogi Bear, everything," Chicagoan Shirley Garms recalls. "I came as a watermelon. Helen Duval was an orange pussycat."

"The girls were always thinking up things to pull on me," adds Wyatt Slaughter. "It got to be a game: tournament director versus the girls. It's friendly and, let's face it, if that helps them relax, it's okay.

"During the Wichita tournament, I was walking through the squad room and I overheard one girl make a comment about a runner in her hose. So I said, 'That's okay, the PWBA needs more exposure.'

"The next tournament was in Tulsa, and at the first squad meeting, I noticed this paper sack with a note that was addressed to me. It said, 'Enclosed you will find your official PWBA tournament director's uniform. It must be worn at all times, owing to your beliefs that the PWBA needs more exposure.'

"They wouldn't let me out of there without showing it to everybody, so I opened it up and inside was a Coors [beer] tee-shirt with a big-busted nude woman and the message, 'Bowl!' written on it. As soon as I held it up, Edie Jo Neal pops up in the back and says, 'I modeled for it!' I looked at her, took another look at the tee-shirt, and said, 'No, the bulges are in the wrong place.' "

Such fun and games during a tournament brings relief from the drudgery of housework or of a paying job, which many of the women hold to support their bowling careers. There have been nurses and schoolteachers, bookkeepers and secretaries, a restaurateur and a jewelry designer, fashion models and nightclub singers, a motel owner, and a retired WAC master sergeant. Toni Calvery is a dean at the University of Oklahoma; Ann Sanders is an exotic dancer-singer with a black belt in karate; Claudine Walker has sung opera.

Though many of these jobs can be satisfying, it is safe to say that most of the women would rather be bowling. "I hate to work," insists Patty Costello, who no longer has to. "I used to work in a potato-chip factory, where my job was stapling packs of flower seeds to the bags and then putting them in boxes. I also sold encyclopedias. When people said, 'Those encyclopedias sure are expensive, aren't they?' I used to say, 'You'd better believe it!' Some saleslady."

Dotty Fothergill too has won enough to support herself between tournaments. She reports, "I retired when I was nineteen. Between tournaments I go to the beach at Cape Cod, work in my yard, bowl, visit my folks. Everybody envies me, but I get awfully bored doing nothing. I think about getting a job, but even if I got paid ten dollars an hour, I know I would think about how I could earn a thousand dollars by just throwing one strike. Sometimes it's hard to get serious about working."

Part of the slack time is filled with practice, of course. Costello keeps her game sharp by rolling an average of 15 games per day. She also likes to join "pot games" with the male bowlers in her area. Loa Boxberger and a growing number of the women complement their bowling regimen with vigorous physical exercise. Boxberger gets help from her three-year-old German shepherd, Keno. "I have to stay in shape to bowl well," she says. "If I try to get away with not running my two miles a day, Keno nudges me to get me going."

"Then there's people like my wife," interjects Wyatt Slaughter about Ann Slaughter, who also happens to be a pro bowler. "She came back from one four-week tournament stretch and refused to throw a ball until a week before the next event. But she did that in 1976, too, and cashed in every event but one, so I didn't argue with her."

Ann Slaughter's low tolerance for sustained top-level competition raises an interesting and important point about women's pro bowling and its expansion potential. Like Slaughter, Betty Morris feels sapped by a few tournaments back to back, and she suggests that the women could not abide a full-time tour, even if the sponsors could be found. "I could never keep up with the pace of a TV tour like the men," she said after one four-week stretch of events. "Fourteen or fifteen straight weeks on the road? Most of the girls, me included, are pooped after three tournaments in a row. Even if the prize money went up tremendously, I don't think we'd be any less tired."

Thus, the women find themselves in an uncomfortable position. On the one hand the status quo of a part-time tour is not wholly displeasing to them. They feel physically capable of keeping only an abbreviated schedule. Some feel an emotional commitment to a job or family that precludes full-time attention to bowling. Others don't expect to earn a living at bowling. They're out there for the thrill of doing something they love, with a chance at making some money at it. They can afford to lose, much like some of the male bowlers.

At the same time, though, the women know they must bowl more if they are to gain the exposure and command the purses they feel they deserve. As it stands now only about thirty women can even afford to attend all the tournaments, few though they are. The more a woman bowls, the more expenses she incurs—expenses not likely to be covered by her winnings. Even the top performers come close to losing money on the tour.

The bowling Coburn clan of Buffalo, New York, for example, has two PWBA champions in the family: mother Doris and daughter Kathy. When Kathy finally cut back on her competitive schedule to go back to schoolteaching, her father (and coach), Frank, endorsed the move. "Kathy's the smart one in the family," he groaned. "We spent eleven thousand dollars one year to make thirteen."

If the money's not out there, then it's not fun for me," observes Paula (Sperber) Carter, the blonde superstar from Miami, Florida. "There is too much pressure because you're bowling for hundreds when you should be bowling for thousands. You really have to be dedicated to stay on the tour at its present value."

At the moment most women can agree that there ought to be more tournaments offering more prize money. The question is how to make it happen. Are the organizational disputes now finally over? Can sponsors be interested in women's pro bowling? And perhaps most important of all, how far will the women themselves decide they want to go? The history of women in sports suggests that they'll go no further than they insist on going.

Loa Boxberger belonged to both the LPBA and the PWBA. Their merger relieved her and all other women bowlers of the uncomfortable but increasingly likely prospect of having to choose between the two groups.

Right: *Looking at a given lane from the
pindeck back, one can see a reflection of
the ceiling lights off the oil dressing on
the lane. This shot shows the reflection
(and the oil) beginning only at the ninth
board (on the bowler's right) of the lane
—evidence of an oil barrier, or "block,"
that will keep the ball from hooking too
early.* Opposite top and bottom: *These
shots were taken through a microscope,
showing the lane dressing (or lack of it)
seven times larger than what the naked
eye could discern. The top shot shows
the hard, unlubricated surface of the
most heavily bowled section of the lane,
the ball track. The bottom shot shows what
happens when oil is applied only to the
ridge outside the ball track—it stays
there, in a neat line, rather than filling
in the groove of the ball track. In
other words, oil stays where it's put,
making lane blocking a simple matter of
putting down the oil in the wrong place.*

5. Dressed to Kill

Oil Crisis on the Lanes

BALL TRACK AFTER 1000 ROLLS

½ OIL ½ DRY-COND. APPLIED WITH SPONGE 4TH BOARD FROM TOP

On a cold January evening in Akron, Ohio, a sweaty-palmed bowler checked the score projected on the screen above the lanes and saw nine strikes marked after his name. Thoughts of ceremonious presentations of diamond rings and belt buckles, his name in the national record books, his picture in the sports pages, teased his mind as he waited for his four teammates to complete their last frame and give him his chance at bowling immortality. His teammates hurriedly obliged, trying not to show their anxiousness. Finally, with a calm bred of extreme excitement, he almost casually stroked his last three strikes. The ultimate bowling triumph was his—a 300 game.

Then his troubles began.

Before awarding its prizes for all 300, 299, and 298 games, 700 and 800 series, and certain other high scores, the ABC carefully checks the conditions under which they were achieved. The local ABC secretary is notified, and he makes an official inspection of the lanes, the ball used, and all the pins, which must be removed from the automatic pinsetting machines and placed in sealed boxes until they can be weighed and measured.

The lanes, balls, and pins all must conform to ABC standards. If they don't, the ABC refuses to accredit the high score. This is exactly what happened to that Akron bowler. In effect, the sport's ruling body called his "perfect game" a fraud. The lanes on which he had bowled the 300-game had been doctored, and the ABC was forced to take action.

A little politics: the ABC, like any other congress, does not like to displease its constituents. It gains its influence (and, indeed, the game its stability) from the fact that it represents millions of bowlers across the country. By refusing to honor many bowlers' high scores, the ABC is in the short run undercutting itself. Bowlers join the organization partly to be eligible for its prestigious awards. Obviously, disappointed and enraged bowlers will be apt to leave, and potential new members reluctant to join, if the ABC gets a reputation for reneging on awards. There have even been instances when bowlers have taken the ABC to court to attempt to force it to grant awards.

There is another reason too that the ABC would prefer not to cross its members: it costs money. The ABC spends more to deny a high-score award than to give one, since denials force the organization to

reevaluate and initiate further verification procedures and training programs to discourage improper conditions. In the 1974-75 and 1975-76 seasons, the ABC spent three hundred thousand dollars simply checking lane conditions.

Why, then, is the ABC doing all this to itself—discouraging its members by denying them awards and spending their dues to check up on them, rather than offering more positive services? The answer is that the game is threatened. Certain bowlers are scoring far too high, others too low, mostly because lanes have been improperly conditioned and, in some cases, flagrantly "blocked" to steer the ball into the pocket. A blocked lane can add four to eight strikes per game, making a mockery of the sport.

The overwhelming majority of games, high scoring and otherwise, are rolled under proper conditions. In 1974-75, for example, a season in which the number of high-score denials rose higher than ever before, there were about five hundred denials to more than thirty thousand approvals. However, a more realistic measurement of the problem—the simple increase in high scores—shows it to be widespread. In 1974-75, the ABC approved 1,606 three-hundred games, 92 percent more than in 1963-64. There were five times as many approved 800 series in 1974-75 than in 1963-64, and more than twice as many approved 700s. Meanwhile, ABC membership actually decreased slightly.

Today's bowlers, like all sportsmen, have better training and better equipment than their predecessors. Even so, it seems clear that at least some of those high scores were achieved under improper lane conditions, which the ABC failed to detect.

Every segment of the bowling community can and does claim limits to what it can do. The ABC protests that despite its vast resources it was never designed to be a police agency. Proprietors cite different economic pressures that prevent them from scrupulously attending to the conditions in their houses. The great majority of bowlers simply don't concern themselves, not realizing that the problem of improper lane conditions affects everybody's scores, not just those of the best bowlers.

Nevertheless, the consensus has emerged among the top figures in the sport that something must be done. In the short run the game may attract more business on the strength of the higher scores, just as the ABC may lose some members by denying the legitimacy of certain high scores. But in the long run the game can only suffer if it, in effect, rewards less skilled players with the scores of experts. Not long ago the 200 average was the benchmark of the expert; today it is relatively common. Once expertise becomes commonplace, the game will lose its challenge for the talented players, and for the less talented it will become instantly frustrating, as they see high scores everywhere but on their scoresheets. Rising scoring creates rising expectations, which sooner or later are bound to be rudely disappointed. The larger the inflationary bubble grows, the more fragile it becomes, and the more shocking the effect when it bursts. Better to try to pop it now, while the problem is still manageable.

First, some good news: The game has successfully met many challenges to its integrity before, some quite recently. In the matter of ball size, weight, weight distribution, and composition, for example, the ABC and PBA have curbed a variety of practices that threatened to undermine the game.

Some years ago, before the advent of the automatic pinspotters, a bowler attempted to use a ball somewhat larger than a basketball. He was disqualified only because someone happened to notice the oversized ball next to a regulation one on the ball rack. These days the size limitations of the pinsetting equipment and ball-return machines pretty well insure that the size of a ball will not exceed ABC specifications (27 inches in circumference).

Tampering with weights in balls, though, is quite common, albeit easily discovered. All bowling balls are made with slightly more weight on one side than the other, to compensate for the weight lost in the drilling of the finger holes. The ABC permits certain small top weights and side weights to be added to balance the ball after it is drilled, since the size and angle of the holes make it impossible to offset precisely the weight loss in advance. The added side or top weight can be a small advantage to the expert, but has a negligible effect on anyone else's game. However, if extra weight is added or the weight redistributed, it can create the erratic but powerful effect of an unbalanced, "dodo" ball, which could give any bowler an edge.

A few years ago some clever players developed a method of adding mass to a ball without adding weight, thus escaping discovery in the pretournament weigh-ins. (A ball must weigh no more than 16 pounds.) They drilled a hole in the ball and filled it in part with barium powder, a metal, and the rest of the way with normal ball-plugging compound. The ball weight remained unchanged, but the weight was now distributed unevenly, for considerably more hitting power if properly exploited. The PBA foiled this practice simply by banning the use of a plugged ball in any PBA tournament.

More difficult to control was the soft ball craze, which started with the now-legendary discovery of "the Soaker" by Don McCune, a talented pro bowler. McCune inmmersed his ball in a chemical solution that softened the shell of the ball, permitting the ball to grip the lane better, especially when it hit the pins. A ball that is gripping strongly drives through the pins instead of "quitting" (deflecting too much) when it hits them. As a result it achieves better pin action and, of course, higher pinfall. (More about this later.)

McCune's was a new idea based on an old principle: the more friction between a rolling ball and the lane, the better the ball adheres to the lane. Oldtimers discovered this in reverse on the shellac-dressed lanes of the prewar era. A soft surface, shellac favored a hard ball, giving it greater traction. On the new, harder surfaces of lacquer and, later, polyurethane, a soft ball gripped better. So McCune discovered; soft balls did score better.

As soon as he revealed his secret, amateurs and pros alike rushed to soften their balls with whatever chemicals they could find. Manufacturers too joined the rush, producing soft-shelled balls and then still softer ones to outdo the competition.

It took the ABC, PBA, and a mechanical device called the durometer, which measures ball hardness, to put a stop to this virtual melting of bowling balls. The PBA acted first, setting a hardness minimum of 75 on the durometer. The ABC soon followed with a less stringent 72. The anguished cries that greeted these rulings could have convinced the uninitiated that bowling was meant to be played with a gumball and that the ABC and PBA were destroying the game rather than protecting it. In any case, the tumult quickly died down when it became clear that the soft ball benefited only the pros, anyway. The average bowler could expect nothing more than a ball that got dirty very fast, could not be easily cleaned, and became misshapen and

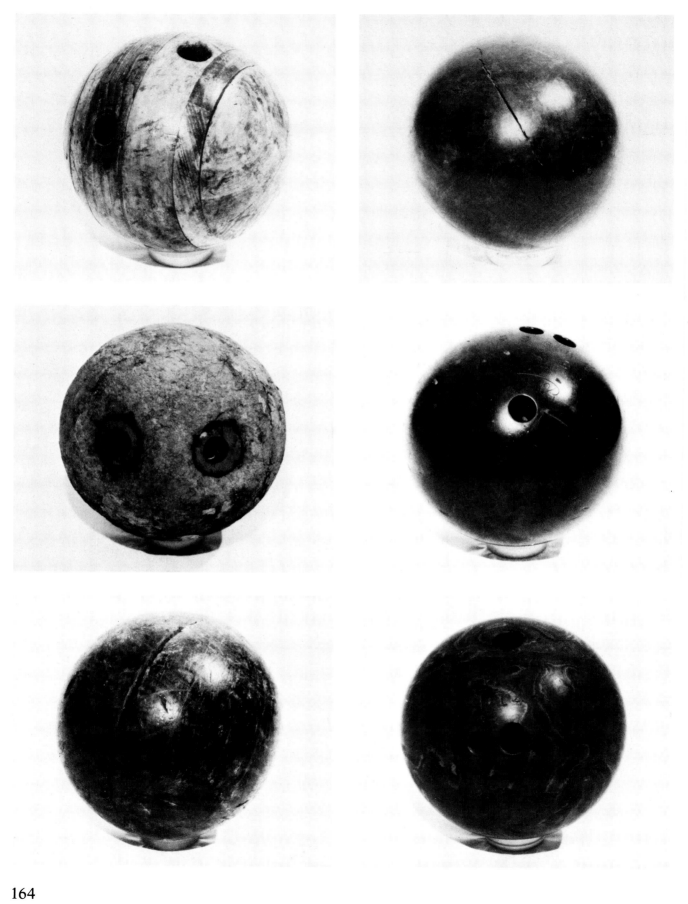

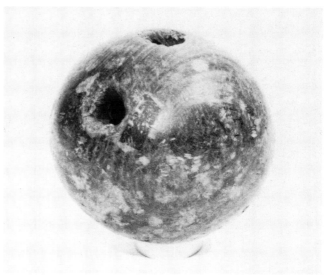

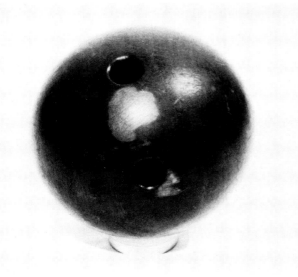

Bowling balls of the past, from the National Bowling Hall of Fame and Museum in Greendale, Wisconsin. Opposite left row (top to bottom): *laminated wood ball, a type that attempted unsuccessfully to compete with the hard rubber balls of the early 1900s; clay ball, only one of its kind in the museum; large ball made from* lignum vitae, *a very hard, tropical wood that was the standard material for bowling balls before the advent of hard rubber.* Opposite right row: *small* lignum vitae *ball (no fingerholes); Ebonite hard rubber ball first used in 1924; ball used for more than 60 years, 1905-68.* Left row: lignum vitae *ball; 70-year-old wood ball; small* lignum vitae *ball (fingerholes, too large for a youngster, suggest it might have been used in a duckpin-like game).* Above row: *cork ball (made of compressed wood particles), used by women and youngsters in the 1930s;* lignum vitae *ball.*

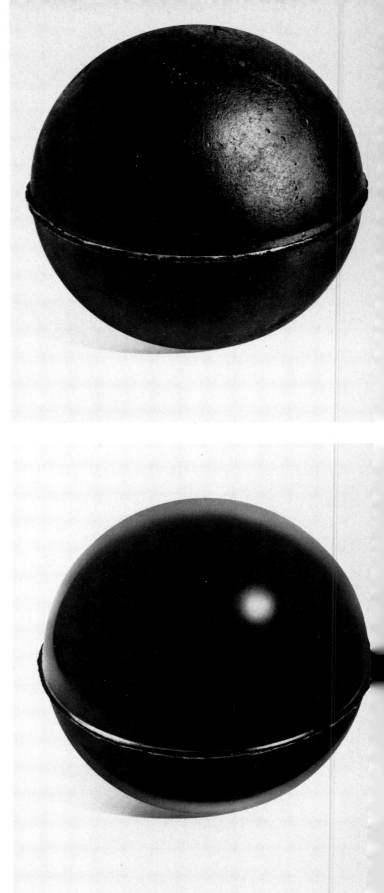

Other than lane conditioning problems, the most heated equipment controversy of recent years has concerned "soakers" —balls soaked in chemical solutions to make their shells softer, allowing them to grip the lane better. When the soaker craze was at its height (before the PBA and ABC imposed ball-hardness standards), the pail threatened to replace the bowling ball bag. Above: backyard sport; left: Barry Asher takes the plunge. Opposite: A bowling ball takes shape.

Right: *These days all pins contain voids.* Below: *stages of the pinmaking process.* Opposite: *The latest AMF process for plastic-coating pins sandwiches them between Surlyn half molds (above) and compresses the molds into a single plastic coating (below). Note in top picture that pins on lowest rack have already been through the compression process and are ready for trimming.*

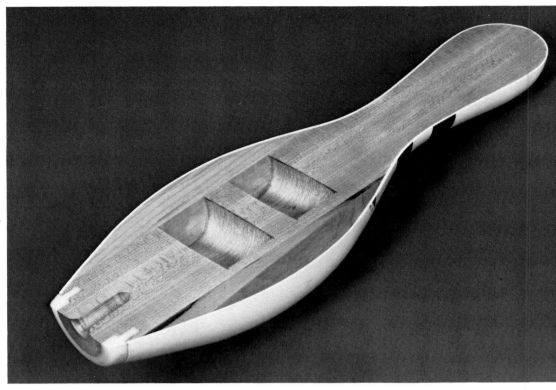

unusable when exposed to even the mildest heat. There the matter rests today, waiting for another Don McCune to discover a less messy and more easily exploitable way for bowlers to increase the friction between ball and lane.

In the matter of pins, too, the ABC has succeeded in preserving the challenge in the game, though there are still some detractors who insist that the pins of today are far easier to knock down than those of years ago. To meet the ABC's requirements, pins must weigh between 3 pounds 2 ounces and 3 pounds 10 ounces, and must not vary more than 4 ounces within a set of 20. (Automatic pinspotters use two sets of 10, to have one always ready for a new frame.) Pins must also have flat bottoms, since a rounded bottom makes the pins unstable, able to be toppled at the slightest impact.

Once, all bowling pins were made of one piece of hard-rock maple, turned down on a lathe to the required dimensions and covered with a very thin (4/1,000ths of an inch) coat of white lacquer. This process wasted a good deal of wood (only 12 percent of the wood cut for a pin ended up as one), and the pins lasted for only five hundred games or so, since each pin block contained the structural weaknesses of the wood. In 1947, the ABC approved the first laminated pin, the block for which consisted of several pieces of wood glued together. This new structure, with modifications still in use today, added both strength and life to the pins. Then, to further protect the pins and prolong their lives, a thicker plastic coating (35/1,000ths of an inch) was added. To compensate for the heavier outside coating, which added as much as six ounces to the pins, the inside of the pins had to be hollowed out, creating the first pin voids.

Pin voids further protected the wood supply, since now it took even less wood to make a pin. But they also engendered a fierce controversy, which still flares up today, over the integrity of the pins. It's not simply a question of weight. A pin with a void may weigh no less than a solid one, but if the void is not precisely positioned so as not to disturb the center of gravity, the pin is likely to fall differently and, conceivably, more easily.

The ABC has exhaustively tested each of its new pin designs before authorizing them, and guarantees that any changes will not affect the average score over a full-year's play by more than one pin.

Although some skeptics have yet to be convinced, the ABC case appears reputable. The dramatic increase in high scores has come only in the 1970s, well after the introduction of pin voids.

As for the future of pin design, it is safe to say that the day of the completely synthetic pin is not far off. The ABC approved such a pin in 1963, but it was not successfully marketed at that time. At present, with ever-dwindling supplies of virgin-growth hard-rock maple, the synthetic pin is becoming increasingly attractive.

If it were only pins and balls that the ABC had to oversee, it could breathe easily. Unfortunately, lanes also need to be monitored, and they have proved most troublesome. Lane blocking, in one form or another, has become widespread. What the bowling community decides to do about it may well determine the future of the sport.

All bowling lanes are made of a combination of hard-rock maple and a much softer and grainier wood, pine. The first 15 feet of the lane, "the head," are made of the stronger wood so as to absorb the incredible pounding of the thousands of bowling balls that hit that part of the lane on their trip to the pins. An average bowling ball hitting the surface of the head exerts a pressure of approximately twenty-two hundred pounds per square inch. Multiply that figure by the 19 average throws per game, and then by the thirteen to fifteen thousand games per lane per year, and the pressure of this yearly "head" ache amounts to six hundred million pounds.

Once a ball hits the lane, it creates relatively little wear on the lane until it hits the pins. In that instant of initial impact, however, the force of the collision is about two thousand pounds per square inch. This, of course, is the pressure of the ball against the pins, not against the lane, but as the pins bounce off one another and the kickback, they strike the pindeck with enough force to again justify the use of maple for the pindeck. The other part of the lane, some forty-five feet from head to pindeck, is made of pine.

All the wood used—maple and pine—is coated with a hard lacquer or polyurethane finish. This finish, in turn, is protected by a "dressing" of a liquid chemical, usually oil based. The oil is applied to different parts of the lane in different amounts, because different areas require greater

protection and because a bowler can take better advantage of oil on some areas of the lane than on others.

Every properly thrown bowling ball goes through three overlapping but still fairly distinct stages as it travels down the lane: sliding, rolling, and hooking. These stages correspond to three movements by the bowler as he releases the ball: first, the forward thrust of the arm, propelling the ball forward so fast that it does not grip the lane immediately but slides along it instead; second, the upward sweep of the arm, which gives the ball some vertical rotation at the start, hastening the rolling stage; and third, an almost imperceptible twist of the fingers, which provides the side spin that eventually causes the ball to hook. (See Chapter 7 for an examination of the release motion.)

The first stage, sliding, gradually gives way to the second, rolling, as friction between the lane and the ball builds up, slowing the ball and allowing it to grip the surface. As the ball rolls, it then experiences the effect of the finger-twist-imparted sidespin. The third stage, hooking, combines with the rolling in a dynamic mix of roll and hook. When bowlers speak of a ball that causes good "pin action" or "mix" of the pins, they are describing this crosscurrent effect on the ball, plowing forward and spinning sideways—both rolling and hooking—at the same time.

The best-thrown ball has just the right combination of roll and hook, for the most explosive effect when it hits the pins. A ball that slides too little will begin rolling and hooking too soon, spending its energies before it reaches the pins. On the other hand, a ball that slides too long may hit the pins too soon after it has begun rolling, before the hook can assert itself and a proper crosscutting action of roll and hook is established. Such a ball may actually be traveling faster than a well-thrown ball at impact with the pins, but its pin action will likely be poorer. The pins will tend to fly away, reacting only to the forward roll, rather than staying close to the surface of the pindeck and mixing with the other pins, as they do when they feel the scythelike effect of the combined forward roll and sideways spin.

In general, then, the more slide at the head of the lane, the more roll-hook hitting power, whether expended or not, left at the end. Oil at the head of the lane helps the ball slide there. (Depending on its speed, the ball may slide as much as 15 feet before it starts to roll.) In helping the ball slide, the oil at the head is also protecting the surface, for without oil a searing friction would build up almost immediately between the ball and the surface, not only causing the ball to slow down and start rolling too soon but also damaging the surface. Both to protect the lane and to assist the bowler, the head of the lane is heavily dressed with oil.

Less oil is applied farther down the lane where the ball's slide becomes roll, which is just as well since not as much oil is needed to protect the surface there. In a word, then, the dressing on a lane is "tapered"—more at the head, decreasing amounts down the lane. Most houses bring the oil down between twenty and forty feet from the foul line, leaving the end dry to encourage the gripping of the ball in its final hook-roll stage.

Pro bowlers understand these principles only too well. They are always looking for ways to preserve their strength, and a well-oiled lane allows them to do that. They can afford to throw the ball relatively softly and still, thanks to the increased slide at the head, get good hitting power at the end. Dry lanes make them throw harder to keep the ball from hooking too early, and over a four- or five-day tournament, this extra effort can destroy a pro's control. On the other hand, the naturally hard throwers may prefer a drier condition, since they are likely to be thrown off stride when throwing the softer balls that heavily dressed lanes favor. Clearly, the amount of oil on the lanes is enough to affect the game. In the television finals of a tournament, for example, many a pro has been disconcerted to find that the scorching television lights can quickly dry out a lane, creating conditions that may be contrary to those he mastered in reaching the finals in the first place.

There can be no "right" amount of oil on the lanes. What suits one style may frustrate another. A proprietor has to try to find a compromise. By contrast, there *is* agreement on the pattern in which oil should be applied—evenly across the width of the lane. Unfortunately, it's much easier said than done. Here there really is no happy medium, just degrees of inadequacy. And here the problem of lane maintenance takes its most vexing turn.

Naturally, oil dries most quickly on areas of the lane that get the most wear. Years ago, before the recent growth of bowling, lane dressings would dry relatively evenly across the width of the lane. Bowlers threw many different kinds of balls and played many different lines to the pins. Today, everyone tries to throw a hook, and almost everyone (i.e., righties) tries to throw it along a similar route —on a straight line down the right side of the lane, over the second arrow to the left of the gutter. Because the oil along this strip dries far more quickly than does the oil in the adjacent areas, a groove, or "track," in the lane results.

At first, the track leads to higher scores. Balls that would ordinarily break too early encounter resistance from the ridge of oil on the left, which may keep them on the proper line (on track). Balls that would otherwise break too late may be steered toward the pocket by the ridge of oil on the right. With more bowling, however, the track widens as oil around it dries up. At a certain point the dried-up area becomes so wide that a ball starting to hook early, as it will tend to do on the dried surface, will not be stopped by the remaining oil on the left. It will go plowing off line. Instead of a funnel into the pocket, the track has then become a runway away from it, and scores can plummet.

Left-handers, who comprise only 15 percent of bowlers, are spared these problems because the track on their side of the lane builds up more slowly. The lane is likely to have been re-dressed with oil by the time the left-side track could begin to affect balls.

Ideally, the proprietor of a busy center should have his lanes cleaned and re-oiled as often as three times a day. Most lanes are lucky to get such attention once a day. After all, lanes that are being serviced are not making money. Most proprietors are content to allow the track to build up as long as it encourages good scoring. The big question is: where is the dividing line between mild neglect of lanes to encourage better scoring, and malicious tampering with lanes to insure high scoring?

Sometimes, it's easy to tell. A lane maintenance person simply soaks a mop with lane conditioner and applies a heavy line about three inches wide from the 1-3 strike pocket back up the lane toward the foul line for about fifteen feet. The lane on both sides of the strip is left dry. Any ball that breaks too early will meet the resistance of this strip and be guided into the pocket. The block makes it possible for just about anyone who can throw a hook to throw a strike.

Such a block is easy to detect, since it places a distinct line of oil on one part of the lane while the rest remains dry. Other blocks are more subtle. For example, in re-dressing a lane, maintenance personnel may more clearly define the track by applying oil selectively to the ridges rather than the trough. To erase the track, oil *should* be applied selectively, but in the opposite manner, to level out the trough. For a few years the ABC permitted such selective, or "blended," conditioning, only to find that some proprietors abused it by making the selective applications in the wrong places, "crowning" the center (i.e., building up the ridge of the track).

In 1976, the ABC reinstated its old rule on conditioning, which holds that oil must be applied uniformly across the width of the lane whenever it is applied. Although this policy takes discretion out of conditioning, it too has its weaknesses, since oil applied uniformly to a tracked lane will *both* fill the track with oil and build a higher ridge on the still-oily sections around it.

In sum, to maintain a lane as free from a track as possible, maintenance personnel must be permitted to apply oil to some sections and not to others. But is such freedom likely to be abused? The ABC decided it is.

This raises the issue of how the ABC checks lanes for blocks. It is, at best, an imperfect process. There are as many as sixty different ways to block a lane, many not difficult to effect but extremely difficult to detect, or at least to distinguish from the normal wear on a lane.

To check for a block, ABC officials use three methods: a visual test, a finger-smear test, and a tactile test. The first consists of viewing the lane from the pindeck back, an angle from which one can see the house lights reflecting off the oil on the lane. Where there is reflection, there is oil. If the reflection is uniform across the width of the lane, the lane has a uniform dressing all across it. If there is reflection in some places but not others, oil may have been applied improperly. In the finger-smear test, the lane inspector draws his finger across the lane for about six inches at a point where he judges there should be oil. If that section of the lane is dressed, his finger will leave a line marked in the oil film on the lane. If it has no oil, there will be no line. By drawing more lines adjacent to this one,

172

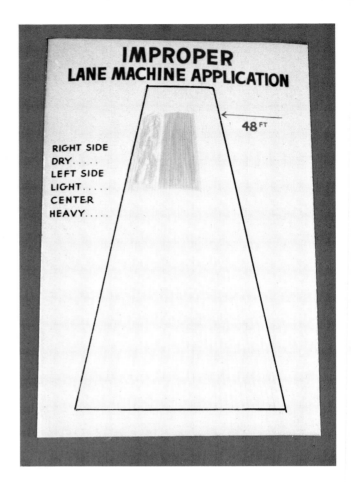

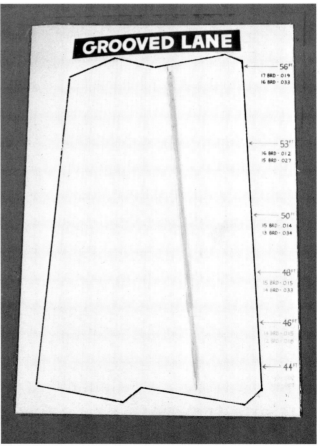

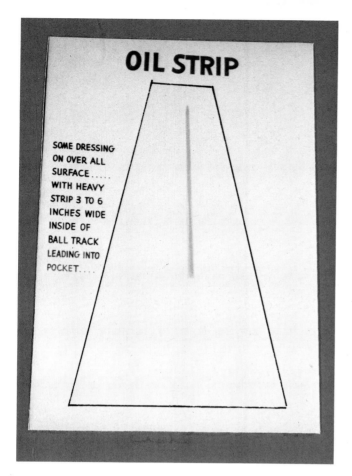

OIL STRIP

SOME DRESSING ON OVER ALL SURFACE..... WITH HEAVY STRIP 3 TO 6 INCHES WIDE INSIDE OF BALL TRACK LEADING INTO POCKET....

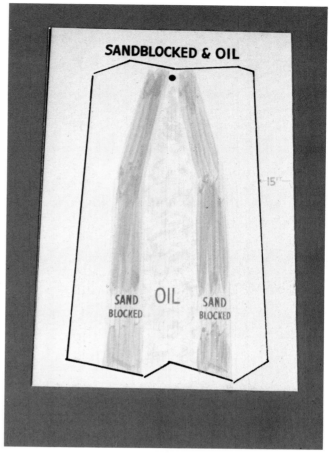

SANDBLOCKED & OIL

15"

SAND BLOCKED   OIL   SAND BLOCKED

CROSS SECTION OF GROOVED LANE

Top row (across): *There are different ways to doctor a lane, but in all these cases the object is the same–to create an oil barrier that helps guide the ball into the pocket. Whereas these blocks are readily discernible, the natural wear of a lane creates another, "natural" block, not always as obvious. A track is worn into the finish of the lane at its most bowled on strip, and eventually the lane becomes grooved (opposite bottom). An even application of oil dressing from a lane maintenance machine, shown in cross section at left, does little to correct the disparity.*

173

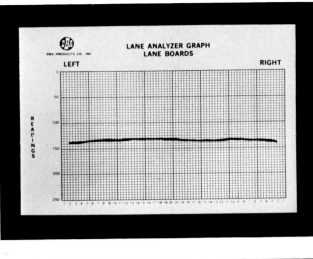

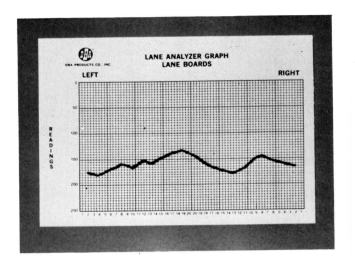

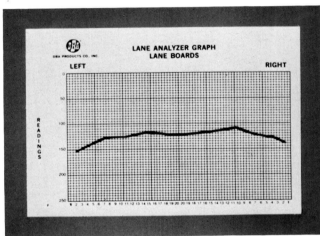

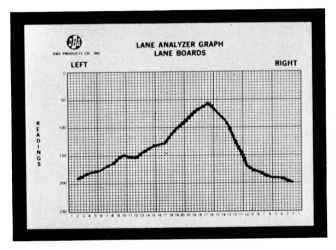

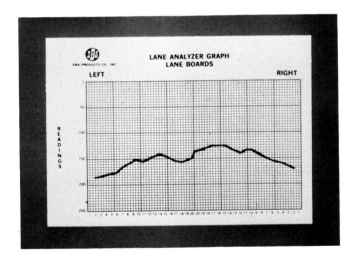

Above: *The readings from the lane analyzer (bottom at right column) treat the lane in cross-section and plot the oil level on it. In this sequence the outside areas begin to wear (lose their oil) first, but in the shot at the top of right column a distinct track can be seen midway between the middle of the lane and the right edge. Next shot shows an obvious block— oil built up in the center of lane to block ball from hooking too much. Opposite top left and bottom: Oil dressing tapers from heavy to light down the lane to facilitate slide, roll, hook. Opposite top right: Blended conditioning can "crown" the lane with oil in the middle.*

SLIDE ROLL HOOK

DRY

DRESSING MEDIUM TO LIGHT

DRESSING HEAVY TO MEDIUM HEAVY

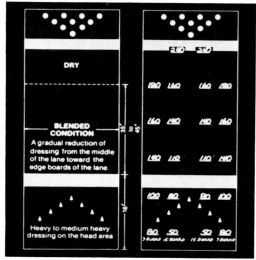

DRY

BLENDED CONDITION

A gradual reduction of dressing from the middle of the lane toward the edge boards of the lane.

Heavy to medium heavy dressing on the head area

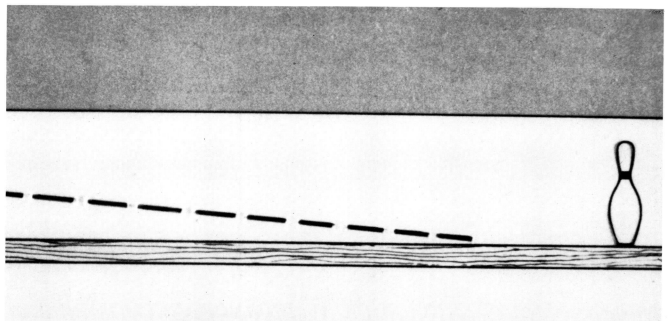

The pin block first became heavier in 1947, with the advent of the laminated pin. Since then, various structural improvements have increased its weight, leading to the need for pin voids. Today, ABC-approved pins weigh between 3 pounds 2 ounces and 3 pounds 10 ounces (with voids) and vary no more than 4 ounces per set.

the inspector can determine whether the dressing is uniform across the width of the lane. If it isn't, he may have discovered a block.

Finally, an inspector touches the lane to tell whether oil has been applied, in which case it will feel slippery. If it has not, it will feel tacky. Recently, ABC lane inspectors have also used a mechanical device, the lane analyzer gauge, which works by checking the friction on the lanes (i.e., the more friction that registers, the drier the lane).

None of these methods, however, has proved infallible in determining whether a lane has been intentionally blocked. For one thing, a proprietor unscrupulous enough to block a lane may recondition it before an ABC inspector gets there to certify a high score that has been achieved on it. More importantly, the ABC checks the condition of the lane rather than the method of conditioning. Its methods don't distinguish between blocks and natural wear, or "breakdown" of conditioner, which can be remarkably similar. There have been high scores disallowed on lanes that were not blocked but only heavily bowled, and high scores approved on lanes that were blocked.

One must conclude that lane blocking is not likely to be stopped by ABC edicts or denials of awards. The heart of the problem lies in the delicate process of lane conditioning, which no regulatory agency can oversee closely enough to prevent abuses. If a proprietor wants to block, it can be done.

Much has been written about the role of the bowling public in this controversy. In particular, the ABC, BPAA, and various bowling journals have pleaded with the public not to patronize lanes that promote unrealistically high scores. There have been fervent invocations of the sportsman's ethic that no game is worth cheating to win. However well intentioned, these appeals are probably not likely to stem the tide of lane blocking. It seems there will always be enough gullible people to make it worth some proprietor's while to promote his house with improperly attained high scores. Once one proprietor succumbs, others seem compelled to go along.

In the end technological advances rather than moral imperatives are likely to solve the problem. Today a synthetic lane surface is being developed that should make the standard methods of lane dressing obsolete. This surface consists of high-

EVOLUTION of a BOWLING PIN

FIRST – the TREE
80 to 100 YEARS OLD

SECOND – the BLOCK
18 inches HIGH

THIRD – BLOCK
split into
PIE SHAPED WEDGES

WEIGHT PROGRESSION CHART

SINGLE PIECE SOLID MAPLE (AVG.) – 3 lb. 5 oz.
1947 LAMINATED (3/10 oz.) —— 3 lb. 5 3/10 oz.

1950
PLASTIC BASE (4/10 oz.) = 3 lb. 5 7/10 oz.

TOTAL AVG. WT. WITHOUT VOIDS
3 lb. 5 7/10 oz.

SINGLE PIECE SOLID MAPLE PIN

USED EXCLUSIVELY up to 1947

AVERAGE WT. 3 lb. 5 oz.

WEIGHT PROGRESSION CHART

SINGLE PIECE SOLID MAPLE (AVG) – 3 lb. 5 oz.
1947 LAMINATED (3/10 oz.) —— 3 lb. 5 3/10 oz.
1950 PLASTIC BASE (4/10 oz.) —— 3 lb. 5 7/10 oz.

1954
PLASTIC COATING – Avg. Wt. 6 oz.
WOOD REMOVED for COATING —— 3 3/10 oz.
NET WT. INCREASE —— 2 7/10 oz. = 3 lb. 8 4/10 oz.

TOTAL AVG. WT. WITHOUT VOIDS
3 lb. 8 4/10 oz.

WEIGHT PROGRESSION CHART

SINGLE PIECE SOLID MAPLE (AVG) – 3 lb. 5 oz.

1947
LAMINATION –
WEIGHT OF GLUE LINES (3/10 oz.) = 3 lb. 5 3/10 oz.

TOTAL AVG. WT. WITHOUT VOIDS
3 lb. 5 3/10 oz.

WEIGHT PROGRESSION CHART

SINGLE PIECE SOLID MAPLE (AVG) 3 lb. 5 oz.
1947 LAMINATED (3/10 oz.) —— 3 lb. 5 3/10 oz.
1950 PLASTIC BASE (4/10 oz.) —— 3 lb. 5 7/10 oz.
1954 PLASTIC COATING (2 7/10 oz) —— 3 lb. 8 4/10 oz.

1961
INCREASED NECK SIZE –
AVG. WT. INCREASE (7/10 oz.) = 3 lb. 9 1/10 oz.

TOTAL AVG. WT. WITHOUT VOIDS
3 lb. 9 1/10 oz.

pressure laminate paneling that is installed on top of the wood surface of a lane. It does not absorb its dressing, as does lacquer or urethane, so it requires both less frequent dressing applications and less dressing at each. It does not track, because there is not enough oil to break down. It can still be blocked with excessive applications of oil, but such doctoring is easy to discern, even for the novice lane inspector. Synthetic lanes may not end lane blocking, but they should reduce it to the proportions of such abuses as plugged balls and round-bottom pins—bad memories more than current threats. Synthetic surfaces are already being criticized by some who feel that in making a uniform playing condition they deprive skillful bowlers of the challenge of adjusting to tricky lane conditions. Perhaps so, but most bowlers, and most officials in the game, should be more than ready to say "good riddance."

Three ways to check for a block—
below: *the visual test, by the reflection of the house lights;* left: *the tactile test (you simply feel the oil);* opposite: *the finger-smear test—where the tracer line stops the oil stops.*

The new synthetic lanes not only look different from the standard pine and maple ones (above—synthetic on the right—and right—synthetic on the left), they are different—just an overlay on the old lane (opposite top). Opposite bottom: ABC laboratory-produced slides of lane dressing and wear bear a remarkable similarity to other slides of similar lane sections shot at an ABC tournament. Note that spraying and buffing in fourth exposure have distributed oil into ball track, but after 1,000 rolls the ball track has all but lost the dressing.

180

BASE COAT LANE FINISH NO CONDITIONER	ATOMIZED LANE CONDITIONER	½ OIL ½ DRY- COND. APPLIED WITH SPONGE 4TH BOARD FROM TOP	SPRAYED & BUFFED LANE CONDITIONER 4TH BOARD FROM TOP

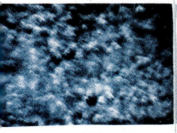 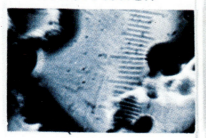 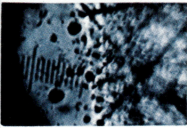 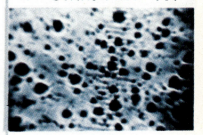

BALL TRACK AFTER 1000 ROLLS	REDRESSED FINE SPRAY IN BALL TRACK	BALL TRACK AFTER BUFF 2000 ROLLS	OUTSIDE OF BALL TRACK

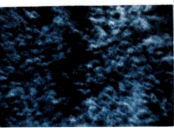 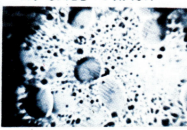 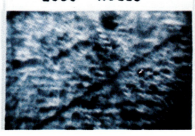 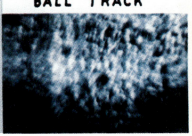

6. The Perfect Strike
Bowling Clinic

Forget for a moment how to bowl and take a look at *what happens* when you bowl. You're throwing a ball down a lane to make it knock down the pins at the end. You do that by hitting the pocket. But what exactly happens when the ball hits the pocket? And what precisely makes the pocket so special in the first place? It's worth finding out, because the principles that govern the behavior of the pins and the ball form the basis for what the bowler is supposed to do.

Every good bowler understands these principles, at least intuitively. The purpose of this chapter is to make them explicit and, in pictures, dramatic. This section aims not to teach bowling, just to reveal it from a fresh perspective. It may make you a better bowler; it *will* make you a more knowledgeable one.

In the picture opposite are the ten pins color-coded to show what happens on "the perfect strike." The headpin starts the line of green pins falling, the 3-pin the line of blue pins, and the 5-pin the remaining red pin. The ball touches only the white parts of the 1, 3, 5, and the 9. (The black line marks the ball's path.)

Now for a more detailed breakdown, building up the process step by step....

A

B

C

D

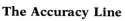

The Accuracy Line

On "the perfect strike," the headpin acts somewhat like the first domino in a row of four: it knocks over the 2-pin, which knocks over the 4-pin, which knocks over the 7-pin (A). This 1-2-4-7 line is called "the accuracy line."

In order for the headpin to begin this domino effect, it must be hit at a spot that is on the 1-2-4-7 line. This spot is at about 5 o'clock (C), and when it is hit, the headpin flies on a line through its center and extending beyond 11 o'clock (approximately), which is where the 2-pin is (D-F).

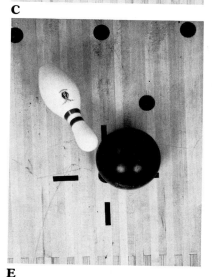
E

F

A.

B

C

Margin for Error

In theory you are shooting at a particular *spot* on the headpin, but in reality you have a slightly larger area to hit—a small box on the circumference of the belly of the pin. As long as you hit that box, the headpin will deflect close enough on the line between the headpin and the 7 to clear out the 2-4-7 (assuming a constant speed and spin on the ball).

If you throw your ball so that it approaches this box flush on, you have more of the box to shoot for (A). You can afford to be off a bit and still hit it, whereas if your ball approaches from an oblique angle (C), the least variation on the line to the box will cause it to miss the target. Put another way, the more closely aligned the route of the ball is with the intended route of the pin, the greater the range of error the ball is permitted.

This is important because, other things being equal, you want to choose a path to the pins that allows you the greatest margin for error. A slight error at the head of the accuracy line (the headpin) gets magnified down the line; the headpin hits the 2-pin a little off line, the 2-4 collision is more off-line, and the 4-7 even more. If you have only a slight margin for error, it may not be enough. The tail end of the accuracy line (the 7-pin) may remain standing, as it so often does on what seem to be almost perfect pocket hits. (The same is true of the carrying line and its tail end, the 10-pin—see next page).

This margin for error factor explains why a hook ball is more consistent than a straight ball. A hook ball approaches at the angle shown in picture B, with not quite the optimal margin for error, but with more than that of a straight ball.

186

The Carrying Line

On a perfect strike the ball deflects off the headpin
so that it hits the 3-pin on a line with the 6 and 10.
This knocks the 3 into the 6, and the 6 into the 10,
wiping out what is called "the carrying line"—the
3-6-10.

The 5-8-9

After bouncing off the headpin, which should knock down the accuracy line, then hitting the 3-pin, which should take care of the carrying line, the ball should hit the 5-pin. The 5 topples the 8, and the ball bounces off the 5 to hit the 9. Pictures B and C show the ball and the only four pins it touches on the perfect strike—the 1, 3, 5, and 9.

Note that the 5-8-9 should behave just as the 1-2-3 does. The 5 becomes the new headpin, deflecting into the 8 as the headpin does into the 2-pin. And the 9-pin becomes the new 3-pin, knocked down by the ball after it bounces off the 5 (the new headpin).

However, even on the so-called "perfect strike," it doesn't work out quite that way. Ideally, the ball should hit the 5 on a line with the 8 (light marking in A), then deflect into the 9. Instead, after bouncing off the headpin and the 3, it travels the route shown by the black line and contacts the pin at the spot shown by the black "X". It's not much of a difference, but it's enough to leave little margin for error in the taking out of the 9. (Technicians who have examined "the perfect strike" have wondered why it doesn't leave the 9-pin more often.) Fortunately, the ball has slowed down sufficiently by the time it hits the 5-pin to deflect more sharply off it than it does off the headpin and the 3. Thus, it takes care of the 9, after all. Still, the fact that it hits the 5-pin not precisely where it should shows that there really is no such thing as a perfect strike —a ball that hits precisely on the accuracy line, the carrying line, and the 5-8 line, and then takes out the 9. No strike ball does all those things.

A

B

C

The Strike Machine

Just as there is no perfect strike, there is no one perfect entry angle into the pocket. What with different speeds and spins, a given angle of entry can produce many different angles of ball deflection. Still, it is possible to show that an optimal entry angle is that of a hook, not a straight ball. We did it with the help of a homemade contraption (courtesy of AMF and Bill Bunetta) that produces perfectly aimed straight balls—and strikes—every time (300 strikes in a row at last count).

The diagram *below* shows approximately the line of entry that the strike machine's ball takes. The solid line shows the line the ball is traveling as it contacts the headpin and where it would be if it did not deflect. The dotted line indicates approximately the first deflection.

Just one problem. This "perfect" straight line into the pocket is an impossible line for the bowler to take. As the picture at the *bottom left* makes clear, it is a straight line that runs right off the lane. To duplicate this strike line with a straight ball, a bowler would have to stand two lanes over. The best a bowler can do is approximate it with a hook. (See next page.)

This doesn't mean that a straight ball won't strike consistently. But it does show that the most consistent straight ball yet devised is, at the end, a simulated hook.

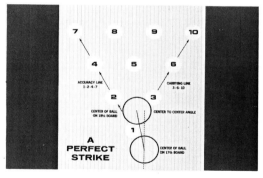

A PERFECT STRIKE

COMMON STRIKE LINE

RELEASING THE BALL

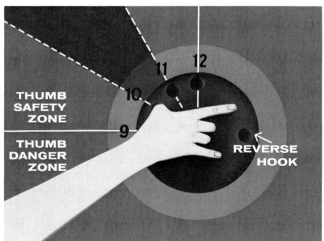

THUMB SAFETY ZONE

THUMB DANGER ZONE

11 12

10

9

REVERSE HOOK

The Happy Hook and How it Happens

The diagram on the previous page shows the line that produces the "perfect" entry angle: straight over the second indicator arrow with a hook at the end. The hook results from the bowler imparting side spin as well as forward force to the ball as he releases it. He does this by gripping the ball with a fairly straight wrist, with his thumb at about 10 or 11 o'clock and with his fingers at about 4 or 5 o'clock (see side-view diagram). When his arm comes forward in the last part of the swing, the thumb comes out of the ball first as the fingers of the hand *rotate slightly*, either clockwise or counter-clockwise. *The wrist does not twist*; only the fingers do, allowing the thumb to come out of the ball first (front-view diagram). Thus, for a split second, the ball is actually resting on two fingers.

The last point of contact between the fingers and the ball is on the side of the ball, not the bottom. If it were exactly on the bottom of the ball, instead of the side, then the upward sweep of the arm would produce only more forward force, not side (hook) force.

Grip Grist

The proper release is partly a product of the proper grip. The wrist must be firm (A), not broken (B). And the hand must be on the right side of the ball (C). If it is on the front side (D), the thumb will release no sooner, perhaps even later, than the fingers, and the wrist is likely to twist, producing a ball with far too much side spin (a curve ball). If the hand is on the left side of the ball at release (E), the wrist is likely to break in the opposite direction, producing a backup ball.

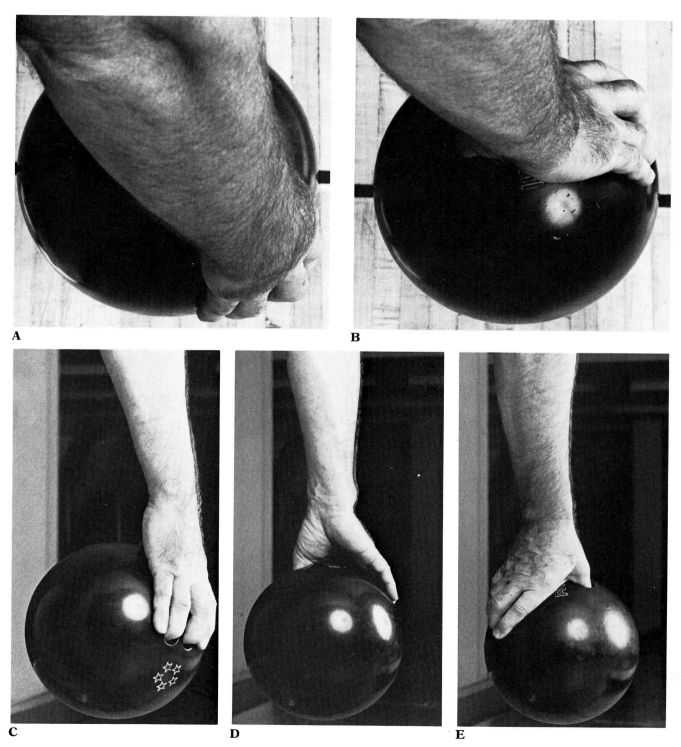

A

B

C

D

E

The Roll of the Ball

These series of pictures show both clockwise and counter-clockwise finger twist at release. Counter-clockwise twist, *left*, caused the ball to roll over its full circumference: a full roller. Clockwise twist, *below*, makes for a ball rolling on its side, as it were: a semiroller. Note that for both full rollers and semirollers the ball does not start rolling on its track immediately. Only after it has stopped sliding along the lane is it rolling on its track. That is also just about the point at which it starts to hook.

A Pin's Eye View
From this angle it is clear that the track of the ball
(in this case of a full roller) only gradually aligns
with the route of the ball.

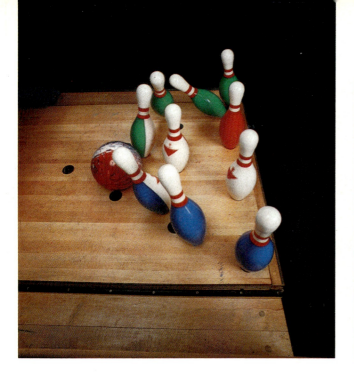

"The Perfect Strike"

Red paint on the ball *(opposite)* marks its deflections. Note that on this, the strike machine's strike, the 3-pin bounces off the 6 and takes out the 9 before the ball gets there. On a hook ball the 3 is driven with greater force along the carrying line and does not bounce back as much, so the ball must take care of the 9-pin itself.

196

Approaches

There are three basic kinds of approaches: the three-step *(top)*, the four-step *(middle)*, and the five-step *(bottom)*. As these series of shots show, however, all the approaches are virtually the same for the last two steps and, of course, at the end.

The Imperfect Strike (a.k.a. "the tap")

This pocket hit, one of a series taken by Lou Bellisimo at the University of Oregon in 1967, looks fine at the start, but just a little deviation is enough to foil the strike. The sequence shows a weakly thrown (though almost perfectly placed) ball, deflecting too much off the headpin, hitting too heavy on the carrying line (leaving the 10), and just grazing the 5 (leaving the 8).

A Postscript on Concentration

A long time ago bowlers discovered that aiming for a spot on the lane rather than for the pins themselves helped them hit the pocket more consistently. The question is how to hit that spot. No easy answers here, just a little surreal demonstration of total concentration on that all-important second arrow.

199

7. Six Superstars
An All-Time All-Star Team

Polls of various kinds have been taken in recent years to try to establish who have been the best bowlers of all time. On these two pages we have listed the results of some of them.

For the purposes of this book, another all-time team is offered, one based on the overall past balloting and a recent solicitation of the opinions of several dozen bowling authorities. For the first time, we present a squad of both men and women. On this roster are six bowlers, four of them men because there are so many more male bowlers than female from which to choose. Arranged alphabetically, this is the all-time roster:

- Don Carter
- Marion Ladewig
- Hank Marino
- Floretta McCutcheon
- Jimmy Smith
- Dick Weber

Associated Press Poll in 1951
for Male Bowlers of the Half-Century
(Voting by Bowling Writers Association of America members)

	Points		Points
1—Hank Marino	995	6—Joe Wilman	730
2—Jimmy Smith	888	7—Joe Norris	594
3—Jimmy Blouin	842	8—Buddy Bomar	503
4—Ned Day	803	9—Mort Lindsey	477
5—Andy Varipapa	736	10—Paul Krumske	454

ABC's *Bowling* Magazine Poll in 1970
for All-Time Men's Teams
Pre-1950 Teams

First Team	1sts	2nds	Points	Second Team	1sts	2nds	Points
1—Hank Marino	27	1	82	6—Jimmy Blouin	14	5	47
2—Jimmy Smith	21	6	69	7—Joe Norris	12	7	43
3—Ned Day	19	8	65	8—Junie McMahon	4	9	21
4—Joe Wilman	16	8	54	9—Buddy Bomar	2	11	17
5—Andy Varipapa	14	6	48	10—John Gengler	4	4	16

Post-1950 Teams

First Team	1sts	2nds	Points	Second Team	1sts	2nds	Points
T-1—Don Carter	47	0	141	6—Jim Stefanich	11	17	50
T-1—Dick Weber	47	0	141	7—Bill Lillard	10	16	46
3—Billy Hardwick	25	14	89	8—Ray Bluth	9	10	37
4—Steve Nagy	17	10	61	9—Bob Strampe	6	19	37
5—Eddie Lubanski	14	15	57	10—Buzz Fazio	7	12	33

Kegler Publications' Poll in 1973
for All-Time Women's Team
Conducted by Jim Dressel
(Voting by 47 veteran bowling writers)

	First-Place Votes	Points
1—Marion Ladewig	33	400
2—Floretta McCutcheon	4	245
3—Millie Martorella	0	243
4—Dotty Fothergill	1	217
5—Sylvia Wene Martin	1	215
6—Marie Warmbier	1	170
7—Shirley Garms	1	124
T-8—Dorothy Burmeister Miller	1	119
T-8—Patty Costello	1	119
10—Emma Jaeger	0	107
11—LaVerne Carter	1	74
12—Catherine Fellmeth	0	49

The Bowlers Journal Poll in 1976
for All-Time Teams

Men

First Team	Points	Second Team	Points
1—Dick Weber (7)	90.5	6—Don Johnson	39
2—Don Carter (3)	89.5	7—Jimmy Smith	29
3—Hank Marino (1)	80	8—Joe Wilman	27
4—Ned Day	50	9—Billy Hardwick	21
5—Earl Anthony	42	10—Andy Varipapa	12

Women

First Team	Points	Second Team	Points
1—Marion Ladewig (8)	97	6—Marie Warmbier	41
2—Sylvia Wene Martin	63	7—Judy Soutar	39.25
3—Millie Martorella	59	8—Shirley Garms	35
4—Floretta McCutcheon (1)	55	9—Patty Costello	28
5—Dotty Fothergill	48	10—Betty Morris	23

(Numbers in parentheses are for first-place votes)

Don Carter

Marion Ladewig

Floretta McCutcheon

Hank Marino

Jimmy Smith

208

Don Carter

(born July 29, 1926, in Wellston, Missouri)

"He looks like a rookie waiter balancing a tray of martinis," somebody wrote to describe Don Carter in the act of delivering a bowling ball. Someone else observed that his right arm, which remained crooked through his release, looked like a "broken shovel." His slouch prompted some people to call him "Chin-on-the-floor Carter." To all of these characterizations he replied, "So I don't bowl by the book, but tell me: who wrote the book?"

Six times, more than any male professional, he was named Bowler of the Year: in 1953, 1954, 1957, 1958, 1960, and 1962. In 1961, he became the only one to complete the Grand Slam of match-game competition, adding the ABC Masters to the PBA National, the All-Star (which he won twice consecutively), and the World's Invitational. He won a total of six PBA titles and 14 independently run tournaments before the PBA was formed. He was an indispensable member of the biggest of the big teams, the Budweisers, and when the beer company withdrew its sponsorship, *he* became its sponsor as well as its leader. The Carter Gloves team won the All-Star team championship in 1961 and 1962, and also in 1962, the ABC Classic team crown as well. He also won ABC team titles in 1953, as a member of the Pfeiffers, and in 1974, on the Ebonite team.

All this from a man who would rather have been a baseball player. "Being a major leaguer was my dream," admitted Carter, a fine athlete who at little Wellston High School won ten varsity letters. "We only had about three hundred students. I lettered four times as an infielder in baseball, three times as a two-way end in football, and three times in basketball." After his discharge from the navy in 1947, Carter became a minor league baseball player with the Philadelphia Athletics' farm club in the Class D Tobacco State League.

"I was signed as an infielder, but we had only fifteen players so I did a lot of pitching," Carter remembered. "I think I batted .304 and hit two home runs. Just two things were wrong: I couldn't hit or throw a curve. Also, I lost twenty-five pounds riding Class D buses and eating Class D meals."

At the end of the season, Carter stashed away his bat and glove and began bowling in earnest.

"I never injured my arm," he explained. "I kept my elbow bent because when I started bowling I used a ball that was too heavy for me and I was afraid to let it swing back too freely." Keeping his arm bent, Carter reduced his fear of losing control of the ball on his backswing.

"So many people told me I'd never be a success with my arm bent and with my short backswing

Don Carter in 1968, some years past his prime. Yet as late as 1974, he was still bowling the best, as part of the Ebonite team that won the ABC's Classic Division.

DON CARTER'S PRO BASEBALL RECORD

1947/Red Springs, North Carolina

Batting	Pitching
AB 96	IP 97
HR 1	H 110
BA .303	BB 32
	K 31
	W-L 3-7
	ERA 4.19

A bird's-eye view of the famous delivery revealed its balance and precision, to the point of virtual symmetry —quite a contrast to the seemingly ungainly shuffle one saw in more conventional perspectives of Carter at work.

213

that I tried to bowl for a while according to the book," he recalls. "That was in the summer of '49 or '50. The results were disastrous. I had no rhythm. So I went back to my way. I overcame the disadvantages of my method by intensive practice."

As bewildering as Carter's style was, it was no less puzzling to many people that he was able to score so well with the "soft" ball he threw. Carter was a six-footer and during his prime he weighed between 180 and 185 pounds, but he learned early not to wing his ball down the lanes. "I found that rolling the ball too fast is a detriment," Carter explained. "When you boom the ball into the pins too hard they don't get a chance to mix thoroughly."

Carter proved his point by often blitzing through tournaments with his slowball. While winning the All-Star in 1952, 1954, and 1956, he overwhelmed opponents in the finals by amassing 124 wins against 68 losses. At the 1958 All-Star, however, Carter experienced an uncustomary slump. A last-day decline dropped Carter from his solid first-place perch and left him 30 pins behind Buzz Fazio as they began their final four-game rolloff for the championship.

Fazio was a showman on the lanes, and that Sunday he punctuated his strikes with leaps and shouts. There seemed to be no stopping him, especially when he opened the first game against Carter with a seven-bagger. Bowling insiders were saying that this grinding tournament, coming as it did only a month after Carter had won the 100-game World's Invitational, was too much even for Don. It certainly appeared to be so. At the end of the first game, Fazio was a 245-227 winner and led by 1.48 Petersen points. But Carter finished with a flurry. He came through with a 236-189 triumph in his second game against Fazio. In game three Carter was on top, 211-168. Then he hung on, taking the last match, 194-193, for his fourth and last All-Star title.

Despite his tranquil disposition, Carter was an extremely intense competitor. He said, "I think being easygoing helped me as a bowler because I never let anything bother me too much, never worried, and didn't let losses haunt me. That helped me concentrate completely on my bowling. There are many athletes of equal ability and I think what separated a lot of them was the ability to concentrate. This is really important in bowling, where

quick reactions are not as important as in some other sports. The pins don't move, so if you can concentrate on how to knock them down you can do your best. Another thing that helped me was that I *never* gave one pin away, *never* gave up."

"Don was the most miserable individual I ever faced on the lanes," said Dick Weber, Carter's sometime teammate, sometime adversary, and longtime pal. "He was *really* cold when you bowled him, nothing like the Don Carter you knew off the lanes."

In 1961 Carter demonstrated his extraordinary perseverance, rallying to win the fourth of his five World's. Laser-like concentration belying that awkward, broken-shovel, Quasimodo, shuffling style, he defeated Ray Bluth in the next-to-last game, 249-223, by closing with seven straight strikes. In the final contest, Carter again finished with seven consecutive strikes as he downed Bluth 258-190. Along the way, Carter set a record for the event by averaging 221 for the 64 games. A year later, Carter again overhauled Bluth, this time with a 238 and a 234 in his last two games.

In 1962, his last big year, he won four of his six PBA titles and tossed a world record four-game block of 1,084 at the ABC Masters. This was also the year of one of his most memorable triumphs, on the television show "Make That Spare." "I got on the wrong freeway in New York, and by the time I got to the lanes in Queens, where the show was being held, I had only a few minutes to practice," Carter recalled. "On top of that, the TV people were irritated by my late arrival."

Carter won the preliminary round that evening, entitling him to one crack at the 6-7-8-10 split and a jackpot worth $17,000. On Carter's big-money shot his ball hit the 6-pin lightly and then thudded into the 10. But the 6 did its job, skidding across the lane to take out the 8 and 7. Carter seldom showed emotion on the lanes, but while watching those four pins go down, he himself went down, falling flat on his back.

In the mid-sixties a knee injury that required several operations effectively ended Carter's competitive career. By then, he had established himself as the single most-famous name in bowling. Even today, well over a decade since he bowled his best, people are as likely to know his name as any in bowling. Don Carter was king when bowling was king, and in reputation, at least, he still reigns.

Marion Ladewig

(born October 30, 1914; Grand Rapids, Michigan)
While growing up in Grand Rapids, Marion Van Oosten was a tomboy who clambered up many a tree. "My favorite was two houses away," she recalled. "It was a dandy." And by the time she was 22, she had established herself as a softball player of local distinction. "I wasn't much of a pitcher," she confessed. "I was more of a batting-practice pitcher for other teams because they kept getting hits off me. But I was a good shortstop. A slick fielder, I suppose. I was also a hard-hitting batter."

William T. Morrissey, Sr., a bowling proprietor in Grand Rapids, took note of her athletic prowess, particularly her strong throwing arm. With an arm like that, Morrissey told her, she could become a fine bowler.

"I had never bowled," Marion said. "There were other girls on our softball team who bowled, though, and one day I went with them to the lanes. After bowling one game, that was it—I was hooked on the sport. I simply enjoyed the game itself and the challenge it presented. But I was never the forward type, and if it had not been for Mr. Morrissey, I would never have gone anyplace in bowling. He gave me a job at his bowling center, he helped me with my game, and he got a couple good men bowlers to teach me a few things. Mr. Morrissey also insisted that I practice *every* day. He always checked up to make sure I had practiced. If I told him I had been too busy to practice, he would take over the control counter for me so I could get on the lanes.

Left: *In the postwar years Marion Ladewig climbed to the top of the women's rankings so often that it became a ritual.* Above: *Her fifth consecutive All-Star win came in 1954.*

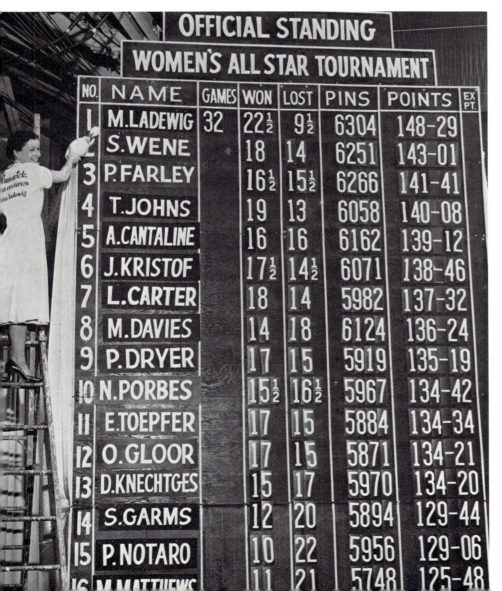

OFFICIAL STANDING
WOMEN'S ALL STAR TOURNAMENT

NO.	NAME	GAMES	WON	LOST	PINS	POINTS	EX. PT.
1	M. LADEWIG	32	22½	9½	6304	148-29	
2	S. WENE		18	14	6251	143-01	
3	P. FARLEY		16½	15½	6266	141-41	
4	T. JOHNS		19	13	6058	140-08	
5	A. CANTALINE		16	16	6162	139-12	
6	J. KRISTOF		17½	14½	6071	138-46	
7	L. CARTER		18	14	5982	137-32	
8	M. DAVIES		14	18	6124	136-24	
9	P. DRYER		17	15	5919	135-19	
10	N. PORBES		15½	16½	5967	134-42	
11	E. TOEPFER		17	15	5884	134-34	
12	O. GLOOR		17	15	5871	134-21	
13	D. KNECHTGES		15	17	5970	134-20	
14	S. GARMS		12	20	5894	129-44	
15	P. NOTARO		10	22	5956	129-06	
16	M. MATTHEWS		11	21	5748	125-48	

With Mr. Morrissey around, I made sure that I bowled every day from 1940 through 1962."

Mrs. Ladewig was a high-strung person, and lengthy tournaments tended to unsettle her. She recalls that whenever she approached her breaking point, "Mr. Morrissey and his wife would take me for rides in their car to calm me down. Other times he would berate me something awful—about being lazy, stupid, womanish, or just plain dumb. There were times when I wound up in tears. Mr. Morrissey used some beautiful cuss words, but he knew how to stir up my fighting spirit and bring out my determination."

As for her technique, Ladewig recalls, "My rhythm was fairly good, I thought, but there was nothing outstanding about my style. More or less, I threw an angle ball with a slight hook. My biggest asset was my accuracy. If there was any other reason for the success I had, it was simply the fact that the game never became easy for me, and I always had to keep working at it."

For her first season of bowling, Marion averaged 149. Three years later she had brought it up to a robust 182. Gradually, she established her superiority in Grand Rapids, then Michigan, and then across the Midwest. Her first notable triumph came at the Western Michigan Gold Pin Classic, where she won the singles in 1940-41. During the next two seasons she won the Grand Rapids, Western Michigan, Chicago *American*, and Central States all-events. Throughout the forties, her average rose steadily into the 190s, and the awards kept coming. By the fifties she had established herself as the preeminent woman bowler of the day. In 1950, she was selected the Bowler of the Year, the first of a record five consecutive times (1950-54). In all she won that honor nine times, more than any bowler, male or female.

Twice she was the winner of the WIBC all-events, in 1950 with a total pinfall of 1,796 and five years later with a 1,890, which at that time was the second highest score ever registered in that competition. In each of those WIBC tournaments, Ladewig also won other championships—the doubles with Wyllis Ryskamp in 1955 and the team title in 1950 with the Fanatorium Majors from Morrissey's lanes. Ladewig also excelled at the two most grueling and grandiose of all the tournaments, finishing first at the World's Invitational four times and taking the BPAA All-Star (later known as the United States Open) a hard-to-believe eight times. Five of those All-Star victories were consecutive (1949-1954), and in achieving the third she averaged an astounding 211.46 for 32 games of match play, a figure that remained a tournament record until 1973.

Her most spectacular string of scores came during that 1951 All-Star, on Saturday, December 15. In her first two games that day she had a 255 and a 279, setting an All-Star two-game mark for women (534). She then added six games (247, 227, 247, 224, 255, and 247) that made for an eight-game total of 1,981 pins and a record average of 247.6.

This diminutive, retiring woman commanded a tournament with relentlessly precise bowling. Others threw more strikes, perhaps, but no one could match her consistent accuracy in sparemaking. "I spared 'em to death," she likes to say. And, as her reputation grew, she "scared 'em to death," too, or so one might infer from the vanquished opponents who admitted to having been unnerved by her very presence.

Still, her almost self-deprecating self never lay far beneath the surface. In 1955, after she announced that she would no longer compete in the All-Star, *Life* magazine reported that supposedly final All-Star in a memorable feature, "An Ordeal on the Alleys." The piece prompted this response from Mrs. Ladewig:

Sirs:

It was a great thrill to see my picture in *Life* this week. . . . Your story was a real salute to the game that has been so good to me. I am a bit worried, however, that people will think I consider 40 too old to bowl and that I have retired from bowling. Although I am retiring from further All-Star tournament competition, I expect to bowl for many years. I know that millions of people over 40 and even over 60 enjoy this wonderful game of bowling and I don't want to discourage them.

It was typical of this, perhaps the greatest woman bowler of all time, to suspect that she somehow wasn't encouraging people enough. As it turned out, of course, Ladewig participated in many more All-Stars and won four more of them. Perhaps it was a need to live up to other people's expectations, not only Morrissey's, that spurred her on.

As a young woman, Marion dressed the part of a bobby soxer but continued to play the role of the tomboy. A strong-armed softball player, she made a naturally powerful bowler, but her accuracy was her strongest point.

Hank Marino

(born November 27, 1889, in Palermo, Italy; died July 12, 1976)

Enrico ("Hank") Marino came to America when he was a 10-year-old boy, alone and with a money pouch and directions to Chicago sewn by his mother into his underwear. His older brother, Jim, had written that he was prospering as a Chicago barber and had sent a first-class boat ticket for Enrico to join him. Marino's father and mother agreed that the future would be brighter for him in America than in the family's Sicilian food and wine shop. So the boy left his family, including six brothers and sisters, and boarded the ship for New York.

On board Enrico strummed his guitar and did a few soft-shoe numbers to entertain his fellow passengers. To his surprise they rewarded him with a few coins. That was the start of a career of pleasing people.

In Chicago, Marino made his money at Bianca's barber shop, first by standing on a box and lathering customers' faces, later by becoming a full-fledged barber. Five years after his arrival, Marino had his own seven-chair barber shop, among whose patrons was Elmer Baumgarten, later the ABC's executive secretary. He continually talked bowling to Marino, and when somebody suggested a trip to the Aurora Lanes one night in 1908, "Hank" went along to have a look. On his first attempt at bowling, it took until the fifth frame before he knocked down his first pin. He piled up all of 11 more that game, for a grand total of 12. Inept as he was that first time, he kept returning to the lanes. Years later, a friend observed, "Hank started bowling at eighteen and hasn't stopped since, except for sleep and spaghetti." It was not until January 1976 that Marino rolled his final ball, when, after recovering from a stroke, he asked to "see if I could roll one more."

Opposite: *Marino, left, with Sykes Thoma in 1916, the year
the pair won the ABC doubles title. Above: an autograph
too valuable to be inscribed on a mere scrap of paper.*

National Bowling Writers Association

Know all men by these presents, that the National Bowling Writers Association, through ballot of its membership across these United States of America, has elected

Hank Marino

of Milwaukee, Wisconsin, as the outstanding

Bowler of the Half Century

Because of his over-all competitive record and his generous contributions to, and his unflagging interest, in the American game of ten-pins for *Forty-one Years;*

Because of his constant willingness to impart his own knowledge and his abilities to all with whom he has come in contact;

Because of his ceaseless efforts to interest new persons in the game which is now enjoyed by 20,000,000 Americans;

Because of his unfailing good humor, his unquestioned integrity, his constant loyalty, his peerless leadership, and his sense of fair play.

Presented to him this tenth day of May, in the year 1951 A.D. at St. Paul, Minn., at the annual convention of the National Bowling Writers Association

_____
President

_____
Secretary

_____
Chairman of Selection Committee

Marino received this citation on being named bowler of the half-century by the National Bowling Writers Association. It now hangs in the Bowling Hall of Fame.

Marino seemed to have an instinct for the game. He developed an unusual shot, one in which he began to spin the ball off his thumb before releasing it. He was able to analyze lane conditions far faster than most bowlers and to submerge himself in concentration. Hank was 5 feet 6 inches and, despite all the pasta, kept his weight around 145 pounds.

Recalling his first victory of note, the ABC doubles in 1916 with Sykes Thoma, Marino said, "I needed a mark in the tenth frame of the last game to pass the twelve seventy-five already on the board. Sykes kept telling me to 'Play it safe. Play it safe.' I did. I threw a big, bending hook and left the dinner bucket, the two-four-five-nine. Sykes, who had been excited before the shot, took one look at that spare and shut up like a clam. My nerves were afire, but I got the spare, and then Sykes and I did a waltz of joy."

At the time of that win, Marino was already 26. For more than two decades after that he continued to bowl on a championship level. If age slowed Marino, it also improved him. In 1932, he and Billy Sixty won what was known as the world's doubles championship, outlasting Frank Kartheiser and Jimmy Smith by 78 pins. Four years later, at a tournament held in conjunction with the 1936 Berlin Olympics, Marino took the all-events and teamed with Charlie Daw and Ned Day for the three-man championship. From 1935 (when he was 45) until 1938, Marino held the most revered of all bowling titles, the national match-game singles championship.

Even though he did not roll in his first BPAA team title event until he was 45 years old, Marino was a consistently high scorer and finished with a 210.75 average over 132 games of BPAA match play. Only one bowler who rolled in 100 or more such games had a better average—Buddy Bomar (Marino's junior by 27 years), who averaged 213.61 for 162 games.

"I was Hank's partner for about fifteen years," Sixty said. "When he began bowling, he held the ball just above his waist and he used four steps. As he became older, Hank held the ball higher and higher, finally getting it up under his chin. He also changed to five steps. Hank did all these things so he could get a longer swing and . . . keep his speed up."

It was not until he approached his forty-seventh birthday that Marino rolled his first 800 series, tossing two in 1937: an 822 and an 833. He added three others in later years, an 811 in 1938, an 826 in 1939, and the last, perhaps the most memorable in 1944. It came on February 17, a snowy night on which Marino left his Milwaukee home with a new ball for that night's league competition. He had little faith in the new ball, not having scored well with it in the few months he had had it. (He had lost his old, more familiar ball in a fire at the lanes he owned.) But because he had not been doing any better with house balls, Marino opted for the new ball. That night it became an old favorite. He put together the second highest three-game block of his life, sandwiching a 232 between a pair of 300s for an 832. He was 54 years old.

Marino was a warm-hearted, sensitive person. He was also a gritty competitor. He showed both these sides in 1937, when he came to New York City for an appearance that almost turned into an irredeemable embarrassment. As the top bowler of that era, Marino was invited to meet the New York press a week before the upcoming ABC tournament. All that week laudatory stories about him abounded in the New York papers. Once he took to the lanes for the doubles matches, however, Marino did not live up to those press clippings. No matter what he tried, he could not decipher the lane conditions. When he left an open in the sixth frame of his first game, a fan booed him loudly. Others soon joined in. "That was by far the longest game I ever bowled," Marino said later. "I ended up with a measly one fifty-four. Then the hooting and jeering increased when my score went up on the boards. This was the most heartbreaking experience I ever went through in bowling."

Then, with the inexplicable magic that such performers are able to bring forth in moments of crisis, Marino overcame his emotions and began putting together strikes—10 of them in a row as he rebounded with a second-game score of 277. "The strikes kept coming in the third game," Marino remembered. "It was after the sixth frame that the crowd began getting to its feet. You could *feel* the silence in the ninth when I left a baby split, the three-ten. I made the spare, though, and struck out in the tenth for a two seventy-eight. You should have heard the crowd cheer. It was as thrilling as anything that's happened in my life."

Floretta McCutcheon

(born July 22, 1888, in Ottumwa, Iowa: died February 2, 1967)

"I was literally forced into bowling," Mrs. Floretta McCutcheon used to say when explaining how, at age 35, she became involved with the game back home in Pueblo, Colorado. "We played in a club and I had been deaf to my friends when they kept insisting, 'You take to games so easily; you simply must take up bowling.' With my home, my church, and all, I didn't feel I had the time. Then they formed a league and, without telling me, put me on one of the teams. There was nothing to do but try my hand before I found myself in club play, totally ignorant of what I was playing at. But even if I hadn't loved the game, I should have kept on bowling. In a year, I lost more than forty pounds, and I certainly could afford to part with them. [Mrs. McCutcheon weighed 211 when she began bowling.] Bowling pepped me up and gave me a new interest in life."

In her first game, on November 23, 1923, she had a 69, and, like many mystified beginners, felt discouraged. "At first, I didn't like the game," she admitted. "The ball curved off to the right side and I wondered why." She quickly learned how to eliminate her backup ball, and both her scores and enthusiasm rose. She bowled in two leagues that first winter and then dropped out because of ill health. In 1926, her physician urged her to take up a hobby, and she returned to the lanes. When Jimmy Smith, the former world champion, put on an exhibition in Pueblo that year, Mrs. Mac attended. His expertise fascinated her, and she began to appreciate the subtleties of the game. Back on the lanes herself, she patterned much of her style after Smith's.

A fellow bowler helped her change. Mrs. Mac said, "My first impression was that the way to bowl was to throw as hard as possible. I stood as far back as I could and ran to the foul line. I often wonder why I didn't break my neck. Then, during my first league season, an elderly gentleman told me to concentrate on hitting the one-three pocket and to be more concerned about picking up spares than strikes. That became the foundation of my game. I wasn't afraid any more of not getting strikes. In later years, people talked about my consistency at hitting the pocket. I think my accuracy was because of what that old man told me."

Remembering that man's advice and rebuilding her style after seeing Smith, Mrs. Mac slowed down her approach, strove for accuracy, and threw a soft ball. She improved swiftly, and within a year after her return to bowling, she had rolled a 300 game and several three-game blocks of 700. When Smith stopped in Denver on his 1927 tour, people there were so excited about Mrs. Mac that they lined her up for a pair of three-game blocks against the old champion.

In the first block on the afternoon of December 18, Mrs. Mac barely lost to Smith, 680-672. She opened the second block with a 246-224 victory. Then, following a 256-234 loss to Smith in the second game, which evened their scores at 480, Mrs. Mac finished with a 224-217 win, for a 704-697 second-block triumph.

Neither Smith nor his manager, Ray ("Red") Bock, made excuses. Smith called Mrs. Mac "the greatest bowler I have ever seen." Bock marveled at "how smart and very accurate" she was. Of the ball Mrs. Mac threw, Bock years later said, "She had a little rolling hook, a 'pathfinder,' that was effective under all conditions."

Two months after defeating Smith, McCutcheon embarked on a 51-city tour that began 10 years of exhibition bowling. Afterward, Carl Cain, her manager, press agent, and schedule-maker, convinced her to establish the Mrs. McCutcheon School for Bowling Instructions. Patterning tours after the then-popular "cooking schools" sponsored by newspapers, Cain lined up bowling clinics for Mrs. Mac all across the nation. Mrs. McCutcheon is still regarded as the most prolific woman teacher in the history of bowling. It is estimated that as many as five hundred thousand women attended her clinics.

She was well known for admonishing her students, "Let your ball roll. Don't try to throw it.

Bowling means rolling." When emphasizing the necessity of following through with the thumb in the handshake position, McCutcheon used to say, "You're just saying, 'How do you do, strike,' instead of 'Goodbye.'"

To encourage ladies to join in the game, Mrs. Mac told them, "Bowling is one of the few sports at which women and men can have such hilarious fun while participating as equals. . . . Since bowling depends on rhythm and timing rather than on strength, women often make more rapid progress than men."

Not everyone took kindly to such egalitarian ideas. Once, while she was conducting a class on Long Island in 1938, a man in the audience yelled, "Why don't you learn how to bowl before you try to teach?" The supremely confident Mrs. Mac responded, "Would you like to give *me* a lesson?" The critic scrambled down to the lanes to take up the challenge and was quickly silenced by the white-haired Mrs. Mac. She beat him convincingly, averaging almost 230.

Lively and outgoing, McCutcheon was a woman of enormous energy. She could teach a full day of classes, then bowl in top form that night. In St. Paul, Minnesota, on December 4, 1932, she spent the day teaching, then in the evening rolled a dozen games in which she averaged 248.2 and had single-game highs of 268 (twice) and 300. During her decade of touring, she bowled more than eight thousand games, on unfamiliar lanes day after day, and yet averaged 201. Her top scores included ten perfect games, five 800 series, and more than a hundred 700 series. Because she did most of her bowling in exhibitions, the WIBC did not certify most of these scores. But she did set one WIBC record, in 1938-39, when she averaged 206 in league play. This mark lasted for 14 seasons.

"Mother rose to challenges," her daughter, Mrs. Barbara Santos, summed up. "She had the ability to shut out all distractions. And she got stronger as a match progressed. She was very relaxing to watch. You knew you were watching an expert."

McCutcheon didn't take up bowling until middle age, and with her prematurely gray hair she presented a grandmotherly image on the lanes. Such an unintimidating role model, as well as her teaching talents, encouraged many women to bowl.

Jimmy Smith

(born September 19, 1882, in Brooklyn, New York; died April 21, 1946)

"Smith was a beautiful bowler," Billy Sixty says wistfully as his memory sifts through the years. "He looked like a swan as he went down the approach, his left arm stretched far out, his right hand bringing the ball way up high on his backswing. Smith was *so* graceful and could do so many things with a ball. He could speed up his arm or slow it down, [he could] alternate speeds according to the lane conditions. Smith threw every ball—no matter what the shot—from the same spot: the right-hand corner. He never even moved to the left if he had to go for the ten-pin. When he went for the seven, he just turned his hand a little more than usual and lifted it. He used his wrist to do so much, rather than move himself around the lane for various shots."

"Footwork is the foundation of bowling," Smith contended. Sixty learned as much when he went to Smith and asked him to give him lessons. "He worked at the Plankinton Arcade in Milwaukee then and I'd get there every day at one-thirty," Sixty recalled. "For an hour and a half he would have me do nothing but slide to the foul line. He would outline with chalk where my feet should wind up and then he'd have me slide, slide, slide. No ball. Just slide, slide, slide. The first game I bowled after he finally put a ball in my hand I rolled a two forty-two.

"Jimmy always wore silk shirts with stripes. Back then, stripes were the thing, and the wider the stripes the fancier you were. But basically, Smith was a quiet person."

There are two versions of how Jimmy Mellilo became Jimmy Smith. One has it that it happened one night in 1898 when Mellilo, who was then a pinboy at Fraternal Hall in Brooklyn, was invited to substitute for a no-show named Smith. The sub led his team in scoring that evening with a 195 average, which in those days was considered excellent, especially for a skinny teenager. By this account, Mellilo became Smith then and there. The new sensation quickly won recognition as the "world's juvenile champion" in 1898 and received a plaque from the *Police Gazette* to certify that title. Word of his deeds brought a 1901 invitation from a Chicago promoter, Nick Bruck, to compete in the Windy City in a series of matches, where one report said he bowled "against all comers and couldn't lose."

The other account of the name change dates it much later, in 1905, when Mellilo faced Johnny Voorhies of New York City for the world match-game title. According to this version, the young Brooklynite was urged to abandon the name Mellilo in favor of one that would be easier for people to remember.

Whether or not Smith was Smith before this match, he was certainly widely known as Smith after it, since he defeated the highly favored Voorhies. A few years later, he beat him again, by which time he had made a practice of drubbing challengers to his unofficial but widely proclaimed title of "the king of bowlers."

Smith proved himself in tournaments as well as challenge matches. He was said to have won for seven years in a row, starting in 1905, a tournament sponsored by the Brooklyn *Eagle*. Smith also became the first to capture two all-events at the ABC, with a 1,919 in 1911 and with a 1,915 nine years later. Above all, he held his match-play championship longer than anyone, reigning from 1905 until 1922, when he lost his title to Jimmy Blouin. Characteristically, he did not protest when it appeared that the pinboys during the match had tampered with his ball to protect their bets on Blouin. Nor did he explain some years later after his shocking loss to Floretta McCutcheon that she had had the advantage of bowling on lanes she was familiar with.

Ray ("Red.") Bock of Milwaukee, who coordinated Smith's exhibition schedule, claimed that between 1916 and 1924 Smith rolled twelve thousand games and averaged 205. Such an average seems incredibly high, especially taking into account the fact that Smith toured the country more extensively than any bowler and must have bowled on thousands of strange lanes. A more solidly documented report gives some credence to Bock's figures, however. It held that during the 1922-23 tour, Smith rolled 703 games, including 16 three-hundreds, and averaged 211.

Like all the greats, he often seemed to lead a charmed life on the lanes. In 1903, Smith met Bill Wernicke in a match at the Randolph Alleys in Chicago, across the street from the Iroquois Theater, which had recently been destroyed by fire. An account of the match told of a bizarre climax: "Demolition squads were clearing the wreckage . . . and during the match their dynamite charges created mild 'earthquakes,' shaking all the nearby buildings. . . . Wernicke and Smith were neck and neck down to the final frame of the last game. Smith had to get a full count to win. He hit the one-three full, leaving the ten-pin standing. Wernicke thought the match was his, but a heavy dynamite charge went off and rocked the alleys with such force that it toppled the ten-pin, giving Smith his strike and the match."

"Smith did all his great bowling in an era when most bowlers would invite match games only on pet lanes," Bock liked to say. "Smith never cared where he bowled. . . . No bowler could read a lane faster. . . . When he was champion, he never backed away from a match the way some others did. And he had that spark of immortality, that ability of rising to the big moment. The greatest bowler of all time was Jimmy Smith."

Jimmy Smith was an Italian boy from Brooklyn whose renown as a bowler, achieved around the turn of the century, had become legendary by the time this picture was taken.

Dick Weber

(born December 23, 1929, in Indianapolis, Indiana) "Richard is the nicest person I've ever met," says Dick Weber's wife, Juanita ("Nete").. "He's always looking for the good in people, never gets mad, and doesn't hold grudges. . . . What I don't understand is how he can get on the lanes and have that killer instinct he has."

Weber ambles through life with the relaxed, unassuming air of a kid kicking a tin can. Don Carter says, "He's very, very easygoing, even more so than I am."

Nete remembers, "When we were given a private tour of the White House, our youngest son—Pete was two then—wet on the floor. Richard got right down and cleaned it up with his handkerchief."

Imperturbable? Not quite. "We took dancing lessons in 1974," Nete continues; "Richard's got rhythm, but he's always too fast for the music and always adds a step, even if it's the jitterbug."

"I guess it's the nervousness in me coming out," Weber explains.

Confusing? The truth is that this Bing Crosby of the lanes is both composed and sprightly. These days he's a distinguished elder in the bowling community, yet he shows no sign of losing the sparkle of youth. He still grins like a kid as he dances (not a step too fast) through middle age.

"A big difference between Carter and me was that he practiced four, five, six *hours* a day and I practiced four, five six *minutes* a day," Weber remembers. "Watching Carter bowl was a lesson. When he bowled, it was like he never knew his opponent existed. After a while with him on the Buds, his ways rubbed off on me because I could see I had to be more serious about my game and about my opponents. Carter had that killer look when he bowled. If I have it, it's because I *hate* losing and because I've tasted winning and like the flavor."

"His first six months with the Buds he didn't bowl well," Carter recalls. "Probably trying too hard. But once he got going, he *made* our team."

"When the lane conditions changed in about '60, Carter and the rest of the Buds helped me change my game," says Weber. "They helped me cut back on my hook and advised me how to rebuild my game. Bowling anchor for the team was the easiest spot in the lineup. You're supposed to be the best shooter if you're anchor, the guy with iron nerves, but it was easy because the team nearly always had the game won by the time I came up. No pressure."

A fair exchange: Weber made the Buds; they remade Weber.

Together with Ray Bluth, he won the BPAA doubles four times and came in second another four. Weber also won the All-Star four times. Three times in odd-numbered years, beginning with 1961, he was the Bowler of the Year. Although Carter rounded out his Grand Slam in 1961, he lost out to Weber in the Bowler-of-the-Year voting because that was the season Dick took five PBA titles, the BPAA doubles, the ABC Masters, a second-place at the All-Star, and a third in the ABC Classic all-events.

When he won the Houston Open in 1965, Weber became the first person on the PBA tour to have three perfect games in one tournament. He did it with a pair of 300s in the final eight-game block. Weber was a member of the 1962 ABC team titlists, the Carter Gloves. Although he has not won the event, Weber has made the finals in 13 of his first 14 Firestone Tournaments of Champions and averaged 214.3, the highest of anyone.

Weber won the second, third, and fourth events ever held by the PBA, and during an 11-tournament span in 1959-1961 was first seven times. He was also the first bowler to reach the $500,000 mark in earnings. Almost from the tour's inception, until Earl Anthony came along, Weber was the PBA's leading title winner.

The first time the two met in a championship final was early in 1976 at the AMF Classic in Garden City, Long Island. Having cut down on his appearances so he could spend more time at home, Weber had competed in only two of the previous eight events on the winter tour and had not won a cent. His weight had risen to 155 pounds, more

The young Dick Weber threw harder and showed his anxieties more readily than the serenely smooth and confident veteran Weber of today.

than hefty for him. Yet Weber beat Anthony, 216-210, in the final of the tournament, his twenty-fifth PBA crown.

And so the question remains: what keeps this man young? He freely admits to dying his hair and popping vitamin pills. "Nete knows a lot about vitamins and she has had me taking protein powder and ninety-six vitamin pills every day for the past few years," he says. But it's obviously more than just physical preservation. Weber still thinks young, like a student of the game.

"Good bowlers years ago wouldn't change their game," he points out. "I change constantly, try to change *with* the game. At tournaments I find out what the leader is doing and I try to pattern my technique after his. I'm ham enough to think I can do anything." In 1969, during a PBA event in Altoona, Pennsylvania, he noticed that he was throwing the ball too fast. So he abandoned his life-long five-step approach and added a sixth step to slow himself down. He immediately tossed a two-game 558 in the pro-am and then won his nineteenth tour title. "I'm a strong believer that excess speed is the number-one cause for not getting a strike on a pocket hit," Weber said after that triumph.

In his later years, Weber perfected his ability to spin the ball early or late, depending on oil conditions. He also became highly proficient at making last-instant corrections at the line.

The more things change, the more they stay the same. Dick Weber is still changing and still staying young. At this rate he may never grow old.

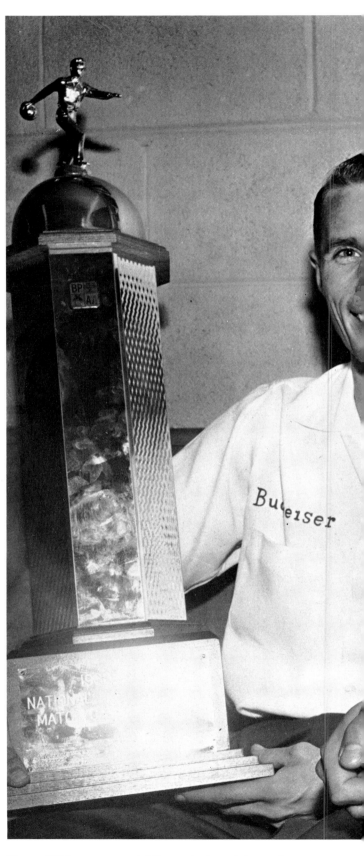

Above: *With partner and fellow member of the Budweisers Ray Bluth after winning the 1960 BPAA doubles crown.* Left: *distinguished elder statesman.*

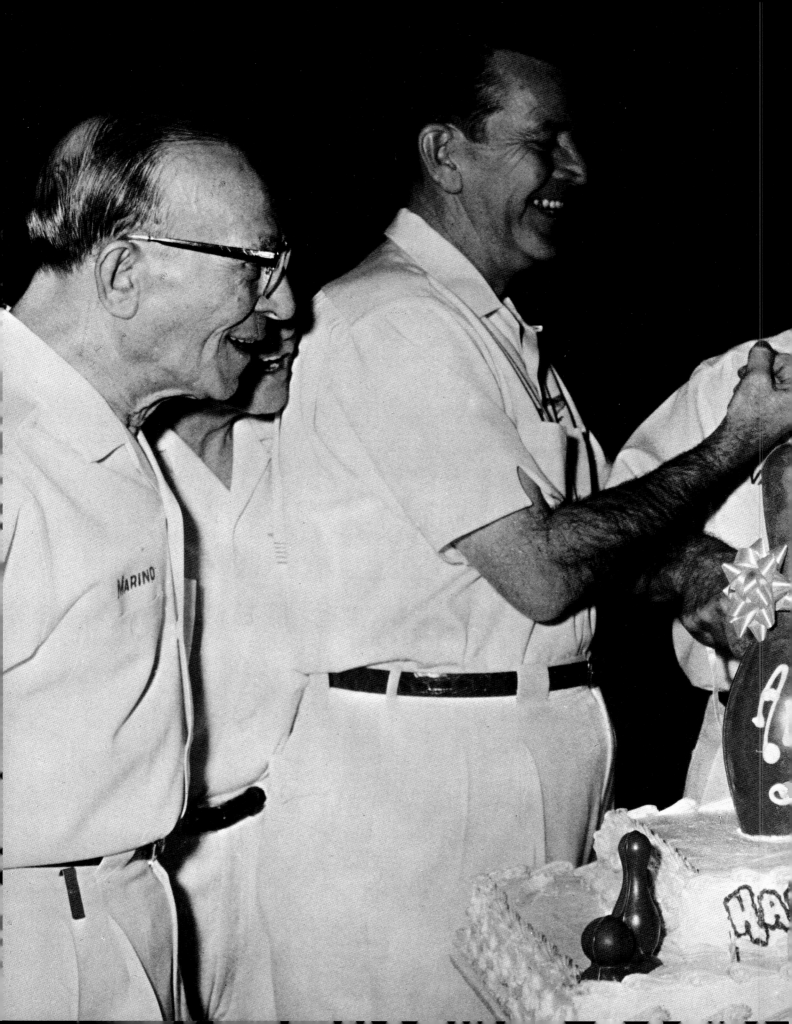

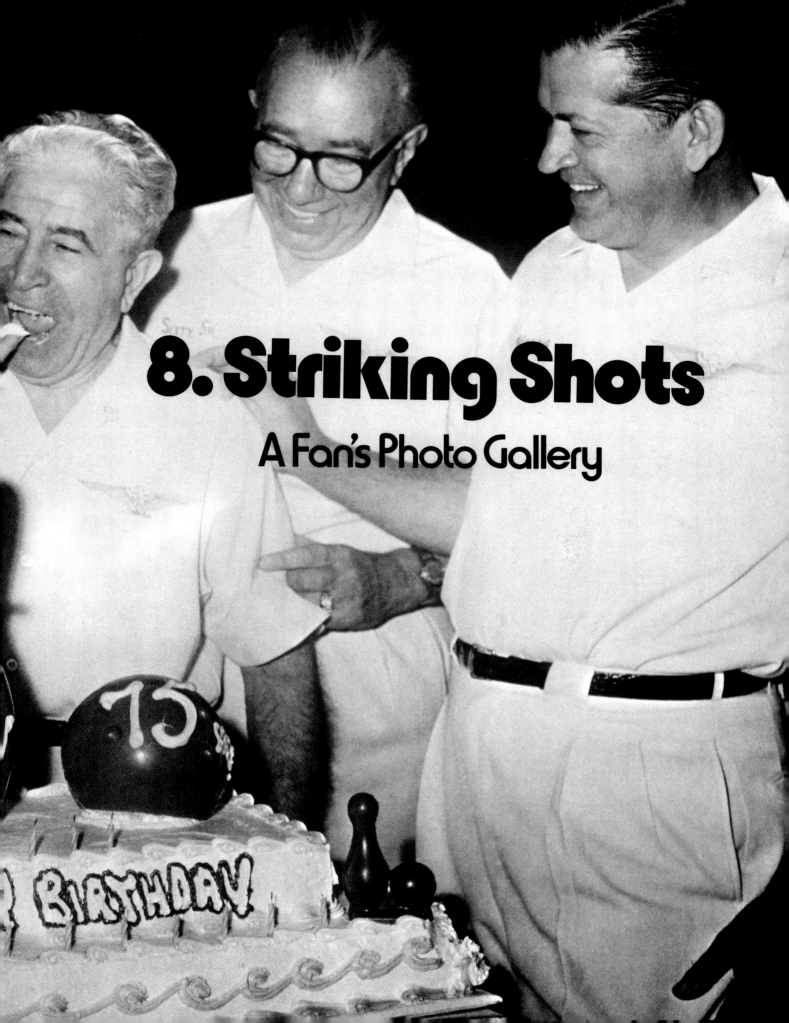

8. Striking Shots

A Fan's Photo Gallery

This book has only begun to tell the story of tenpin bowling. From the mysteries of the game's antiquity to the techniques of today's pros, there is much more of this most common yet most underpublicized sport still to be covered, and uncovered. These few pages may be viewed as a pictorial epilogue of sorts, a place to recognize a few more of bowling's more distinctive personalities. There are some old-timers, some modern stars, and, fittingly on the opening spread, bowling's grand old man, who spans most of the eras of bowling in America—Andy Varipapa. This section intends to be a bit like that cake in the picture—not a full-scale banquet of bowling fare, just a little dessert.

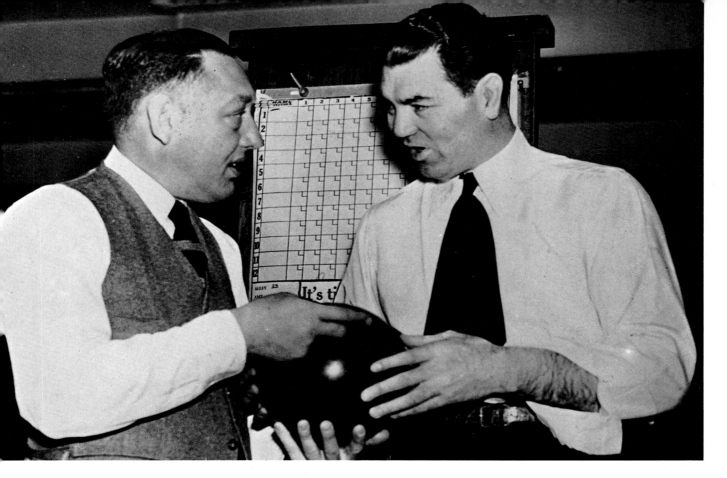

Overleaf—*left to right:
Hank Marino, Buddy Bomar,
Varipapa, Billy Sixty,
and Joe Norris.* Clockwise
from opposite top: *some bowlers
and celebs from the era
when bowling was a
celeb's game*—Frank Kart-
heiser; Mort Lindsey and
Jack Dempsey; Joe E. Brown
and Elmer O'Brien;
Herb Freitag and Bob Hope.

Opposite: *Ray Bluth in the unique chin-to-ball stance he made famous.* Above: *Al Savas firing away for Falstaff.* Right: *Ed Lubanski chomping a victory cigar at the 1959 ABC tourney.*

The sublime at the line–clockwise from opposite: Billy Hardwick coils for the strike; Bob Strampe tries levitation; a young and frisky Carmen Salvino; Steve Nagy, a heavy man light on his feet in anticipation; Billy Welu, a big man extended but composed–classic form.

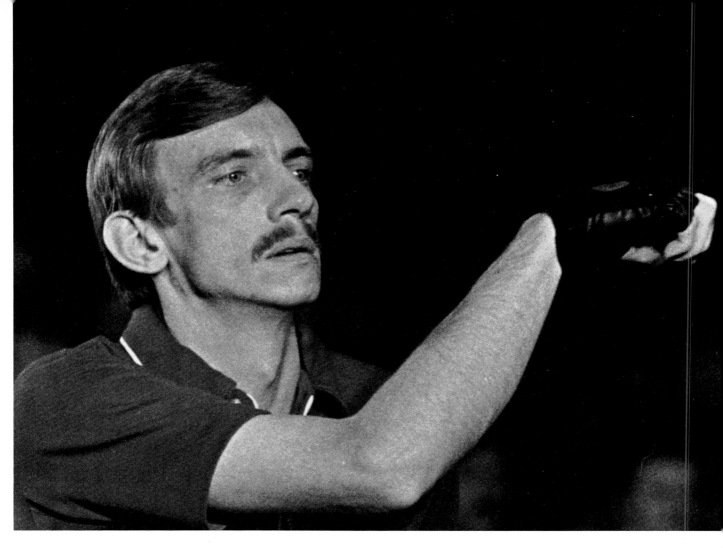

Faces on the tour today—clockwise from opposite right: *Dick Ritger, rarely demonstrative but usually quite content; Jim Godman finishes with a flourish; Johnny Petraglia, no longer a child prodigy but still a young veteran; Roy Buckley looking as if he might be a magician pulling a rabbit out of a hat rather than a bowler with a strike in the bag.*

Glossary

Alley Playing surface on which balls are rolled and pins placed. Also called a "lane." Plural form can refer to a bowling center.

Anchor Last bowler in a team's lineup

Approach Area of the lane up to the foul line; a bowler's path leading to his delivery.

Arrows Markers embedded in a lane that serve as aiming points

Baby Split The 2-7 or 3-10. Also called a "Murphy."

Backup Right hander's ball that falls away to the right; a left hander's ball that falls away to the left.

Balk Incomplete approach without delivering the ball. Interfering with another bowler's approach or causing him to stop or fail to complete it in his usual way.

Ball Rack Resting place for the ball before it is rolled and after it is returned from the pit

Barmaid Hidden pin. Also a "sleeper."

Bed One lane or alley

Bedposts The 7-10 split. Also "fence posts," "goal posts," "snake eyes," and "mule ears."

Big Ears The 4-6-7-10 split. Also the "big four" and "double pinochle."

Block Series of games: ex., *They rolled a four-game block.*

Blocked Track created on an alley by use of oil or lane conditioner

Boards Strips of wood that make up a lane

Box A frame, ten of which constitute a game

Bridge Distance between finger holes on a bowling ball

Brooklyn Right hander's ball that hits left of the head pin; the "Jersey side"

Bucket The 2-4-5-8 leave for a right hander, the 3-5-6-9 for a left hander. Also called a "dinner pail."

CC 200 game

Cheesecakes Lanes on which it is easy to get strikes

Cherry Knocking down the front pin or pins on a spare leave, but missing an adjacent pin or pins. Also known as "chopping."

Christmas Tree The 3-7-10 leave for a right hander, the 2-7-10 for a left hander. Also "Faith, Hope and Charity."

Cincinnati The 8-10 split

Clean Game Scoring a strike or spare in each frame

Clothesline The 1-2-4-7 or 1-3-6-10 leaves

Count Number of pins toppled with the first ball of each frame

Cranker Bowler who throws a wide-hooking ball

Crossover A ball that crosses to the left of the headpin for right-handers, to the right of the headpin for lefties

Deflection The altered path of the ball after it hits a pin

Dime Store The 5-10 split. Also a "Woolworth."

Double Two consecutive strikes

Drive Old name (dating back to the 1800s) for a lane

Dutch 200 Rolling a 200 game by alternately making strikes and spares

Error Failing to convert a spare

Fill Pins knocked down with the first ball of a frame following a spare

Fit Split Split in which it is possible for the ball to hit both pins

Flat Ball Ball that does little; a dud

Foul Delivery in which a bowler touches or goes past the foul line

Foul Line Dark marking that se arates the end of the approach from the head of the lane

Foundation Ninth-frame strike

Frame One-tenth of a game

Fudge ball Weak shot

Full Roller Ball that rolls over its full circumference

Grandma's Teeth The 4-7-9-10 leave.

Graveyards Difficult lanes to score on: the toughest pair in a house; an entire establishment noted for low scores. Also called "brickyards."

Greek Church Split with "three steeples" (the 6-9-10) on one side and "two steeples" on the other (the 4-7)

Gutterball Shot that drops off the lanes and into a channel (gutter) on either side of the lane

Handicap Pins added to a bowler's score to equalize competition. The lower a bowler's average, the higher his handicap so he will have an opportunity to beat a high-average roller.

Head Pin No. 1 pin; the "king pin"

High Hit When the ball strikes the headpin at its middle

Hole The 1-2 pocket for lefties; the 1-3 pocket for righties

Hook A ball that breaks sharply to the left for a righty, to the right for a lefty

House Bowling establishment

Jersey Side Left of the head pin

Kickback Dividers separating one lane from another at the pit end

Kresge The 5-7 split

Lane Playing surface. Also an "alley".

Leadoff First bowler in a team's lineup

Leave Pins left standing after the first ball of a frame

Lift Upward motion applied to the ball with the fingers at release

Light Hit Ball that hits right of the 1-3 pocket for a right hander or to the left of the 1-2 pocket for a left hander. Also referred to as a "thin hit" or a "low hit."

Lily The 5-7-10 split; also "Three Stooges."

Line Path of a ball; a game

Lineage Number of games bowled at a house

Lofting Releasing the ball so it lands well down the lane

Maples Pins

Mark Strike or spare

Match Play Two bowlers competing against one another

Mother-in-Law The 7-pin

Open Frame without a strike or spare

Outside Extreme left or right side of a lane

Pilgrim Ball Weak shot; an "early settler"

Pitch Angle of the holes drilled in a ball

Pocket For right handers, an area between the 1 and 3 pins; for left handers between the 1 and 2 pins. The best place to have the ball hit to get a strike.

Poison Ivy The 3-6-10 leave

Pot Game Contest in which bowlers ante up an agreed-upon sum, all or most of which goes to the high scorer

Punch Out To end a game by striking out on the last three or more shots

Rap Solid pocket hit but one pin remains upright

Reading Lanes Determining the subtle variations of alleys: where a track is, where dry and oily spots are, finding how much or how little an alley affects various shots

Reverse Severe backup

Runway Approach

Sandbagger Bowler who deliberately keeps scores down to get a higher handicap, which is then exploitable by adding those pins when he bowls as well as he can

Schleifer Thin strike in which the pins fall slowly

Scratch Nonhandicap bowling; a bowler's actual score

Slotted House Lanes on which it is easy to roll above average scores

Span Distance between the thumb and finger holes on a ball

Spare Toppling all ten pins with two balls in one frame

Splasher Strike in which the pins fall quickly

Split Pins left after the first shot of a frame, with a gap between them greater than the width of the ball

Strike Knocking down all ten pins with the first roll in a frame

String Succession of strikes

Tap When an apparent strike-ball leaves one pin standing

Three Stooges The 5-7-10 leave. Also called "Hart Schaffner & Marx."

Thunder in the Building Ball that rolls over thumbholes and makes a thumping sound. The shot itself is called a "holy roller."

Track Path worn into a lane by the rolling of many balls in the same area.

Turkey Three consecutive strikes

Washout The 1-2-10 or 1-2-4-10 leaves

Statistics

ABC/WIBC Individual Records

Most Sanctioned 300s

    ABC—26 Elvin Mesger, Sullivan, Missouri
          19 Dave Soutar, Kansas City, Missouri
          17 George Billick, Old Forge, Pennsylvania
          17 Dick Weber, St. Louis, Missouri
    WIBC—4 Bev Ortner, Tucson, Arizona
          4 Betty Morris, Stockton, California

Most Sanctioned 300s in One Season

    8 Elvin Mesger, Sullivan, Missouri (1966-67)
      Ronnie Graham, Louisville, Kentucky (1974-75)

Longest Time Between First and Last 300

    44 years Fred Wolf, Detroit, Michigan, 1931 and 1975

Youngest to Roll 300

    ABC— Matt Throne, Milbrae, California, 12 years, 7 months (AJBC)
        Dale Mesenbrink, Milwaukee, Wisconsin, 12 years, 8 months, 27 days
        Dave Razzari, San Mateo, California, 13 years, 2 months, 17 days
    WIBC— Three seventeen-year-olds (WIBC does not ask for birth dates on its record sheets) rolled perfect games: Nancy Hall of Sacramento, California, Robin Hampton of Richmond, Virginia, and Nikki Gianulias of Valejos, California.

Lowest Three-Game Series with a 300

    530 Jim Albanese, Allentown, Pennsylvania, October 11, 1951 (114-300-116)
    536 Harry Wilson, Bettendorf, Iowa, November 29, 1940 (111-125-300)

Right-handed and Left-handed 300s

    Neal Bayes, St. Louis, Missouri, age 14, on December 5, 1963, while bowling right-handed; June 20, 1970, while bowling left-handed

Average, Highest for League Season

    ABC—239.43 James Lewis, Schenectady, New York, 1975-76
    WIBC—222 Barbara Thorberg, Florissant, Missouri, 1974-75

Crossover Strikes, Most Consecutive

    ABC—16 Leon Kloeppner, New Haven, Connecticut, 1976
    WIBC—10 Thelma Courdier, Tucson, Arizona, 1972-73

Highest Score in First Game Ever Bowled

    ABC—253 Rollie ("Bud") Terrell, Bloomfield, Iowa, August 28, 1974
    No WIBC record kept

Largest League

    ABC—80 teams Moslem Shrine League, Detroit, Michigan
    WIBC—64 teams The Women's League, Downey, California

Longest Stretch Without an Open Frame

    ABC—244 Merrill Weaver, Columbus, Ohio, 1944
    No WIBC record kept

Spares, Most Consecutive

    ABC—30 Howard P. Glover, San Francisco, California, August 1944
        Charles Claybaugh, Anderson, Indiana, January 11, 1952
        Ray Wachholz, Oshkosh, Wisconsin, January 17, 1974
    WIBC—27 Joan Taylor, Syracuse, New York, 1973-74

Strikes, Most Consecutive

    ABC—33 John Pezzin, Toledo, Ohio, March 4, 1976 (9 strikes 300-300)
    WIBC—18 Georgene Cordes, Bloomington, Minnesota, 1970-71

Victories, Most Consecutive by a Team

    ABC—84 Frank Leonoros, Moose League, Charleston, West Virginia, 1948-49
        72 Lefties, Bauer 750 League, Milwaukee, Wisconsin, 1955-56
    WIBC—54 Ed Raatz Inn, Tuesday Ladies League, Milwaukee, Wisconsin, 1972

Youngest to Win an ABC or WIBC Event

    Harold Allen, Detroit, Michigan, 18, teamed with his brother Ray to win the ABC doubles in 1915.
    Lauri Nichols, Island Lake, Illinois, 18, won the all-events at the 1971 WIBC.

3-10 Split Conversions, Most Consecutive

    ABC—8 Francis Barger, Salisbury, North Carolina, 1961
    No WIBC record kept

200 Games, Most Consecutive

    ABC—62 Alfie Cohn, Chicago, Illinois, 1970-71
    No WIBC record kept

298 Games, Lifetime

    ABC—4 Paul Marian, Chicago, Illinois
        Elvin Mesger, Sullivan, Missouri
        Truss White, Ft. Worth, Texas
    No WIBC record kept

299 Games, Lifetime

    ABC—11 Elvin Mesger, Sullivan, Missouri
        7 Dick Weber, St. Louis, Missouri
        Emil Siperke, Cleveland, Ohio

Charles ("Casey") Jones, Plymouth, Wisconsin
Barry Asher, Costa Mesa, California
No WIBC record kept

600 Series, Most Consecutive

ABC—47   John Sabo, Detroit, Michigan, 1954. After ending the streak with a 592, Sabo rolled eight straight 600s.

WIBC—22   Maureen Harris, Madison, Wisconsin, 1970-71

700 Series, Most in One Season

ABC—72   Arlo Heiland, St. Louis, Missouri, who bowled in 13 leagues in 1962-63

No WIBC record kept

700 Series, Most Consecutive

ABC—12   Nelson Burton, Jr., St. Louis, Missouri, 1962-63

No WIBC record kept

800 Series, Most in One Season

ABC—6   Elvin Mesger, Sullivan, Missouri, 1966-67, 834-837-846-825-801-804

WIBC—1   Bev Ortner, Tucson, Arizona, 1968-69   818

Doris Coburn, Buffalo, New York, 1973-74   813

Eva Schutt, Tucson, Arizona, 1973-74   811

Virginia Norton, Whittier, California, 1975-76   808

Mary Cummings, Vestal, New York 1974-75   805

Sue Sewell, Houston, Texas, 1972-73   804

800 Series, Lifetime

ABC—21   Elvin Mesger, Sullivan, Missouri

11   Charles ("Casey") Jones, Plymouth, Wisconsin

8   Nelson Burton, Jr., St. Louis, Missouri

WIBC—1   (same as for one season)

2000 All-Events, Lifetime

ABC—6   Hank Marino, Milwaukee, Wisconsin

Adolph Carlson, Chicago, Illinois

John Crimmins, Detroit, Michigan

5   Joe Wilman, Chicago, Illinois

Frank Benkovic, Milwaukee, Wisconsin

4   Joe Norris, Detroit, Michigan

Junior Powell, Toledo, Ohio

WIBC—1   Dotty Fothergill, Cranston, Rhode Island, 1967-68

Betty Kuczynski, Chicago, Illinois, 1969-70

Olga Gloor, Vista, California, 1964-65

Shirley Garms, Island Lake, Illinois, 1960-61

Pam Rutherford, Oroville, California, 1975-76

ABC Classic Division Singles Champions

		Score
1961	Earl Johnson	733
1962	Bob Poole	759
1963	Tom Hennessey	732

1964	Bill Hardwick	730
1965	Bob Kennicutt	697
1966	Les Schissler	760
1967	Lou Mandragona	736
1968	Dave Davis	741
1969	Nelson Burton, Jr.	732
1970	Glenn Allison	730
1971	Victor Iwlew	750
1972	Teata Semiz	754
1973	Nelson Burton, Jr.	724
1974	Ed DiTolla	747
1975	Les Zikes	710
1976	Jim Schroeder	750
1977	Mickey Higham	801

WIBC Open Singles Champions

		Score
1969	Joan Bender	690
1970	Dorothy Fothergill	695
1971	Mary Scruggs	698
1972	D. D. Jacobson	737
1973	Bobbie Buffaloe	706
1974	Shirley Garms	702
1975	Barbara Leicht	689
1976	Beverly Shonk	686
1977	Akiko Yamaga	714

ABC Classic Division Doubles Champions

		Score
1961	Don Ellis (678), Joe Kristof (653)	1,331
1962	Glenn Allison (780), Dick Hoover (651)	1,431
1963	Joe Joseph (728), Billy Golembiewski (650)	1,378
1964	Hal Jolley (627), Bob Strampe (728)	1,355
1965	Larry Oakar (667), Bill Beach (688)	1,355
1966	Jim Stefanich (753), Andy Rogoznica (608)	1,361
1967	Norm Meyers (757), Harry Smith (665)	1,422
1968	Bill Tucker (697), Don Johnson (632)	1,329
1969	Don McCune (734), Jim Stefanich (621)	1,355
1970	Dave Soutar (747), Nelson Burton, Jr. (684)	1,431
1971	Barry Warshafsky (635), Bill Zuben (722)	1,357
1972	Carmen Salvino (647), Barry Asher (719)	1,366
1973	Bobby Cooper (661), George Pappas (678)	1,339
1974	Tye Critchlow (693), Bob Perry (666)	1,359
1975	Marty Piraino (772), Bill Bunetta (620)	1,392
1976	Don Johnson (771), Paul Colwell (671)	1,442
1977	Frank Werman (748), Randy Neal (589)	1,337

WIBC Open Doubles Champions

		Score
1969	Gloria Simon-Judy Soutar	1,315
1970	Gloria Simon-Judy Soutar	1,256
1971	Dorothy Fothergill-Mildred Martorella	1,263
1972	Judy Roberts-Betty Remmick	1,247

243

1973	Mildred Martorella-Dorothy Fothergill	1,238
1974	Carol Miller-Jane Leszczynski	1,313
1975	Jennette James-Dawn Raddatz	1,234
1976	Georgene Cordes-Shirley Sjostrom	1,232
	Debbie Rainone-Eloise Vacco	1,232
1977	Ozella Houston-Dorothy Jackson	1,234

1969	Larry Lichstein	2,060
1970	Bob Strampe	2,043
1971	Gary Dickinson	2,000
1972	Teata Semiz	1,994
1973	Jimmy Mack	1,994
1974	Jim Godman	2,184
1975	Bill Beach	1,993
1976	Gary Fust	2,050
1977	Dick Ritger	1,964

ABC Classic Division Team Champions

		Score
1961	Brentwood Bowl, San Francisco	5,983
1962	Don Carter Glove, St. Louis	6,248
1963	California Bombers, Los Angeles	6,233
1964	Falstaff Beer, St. Louis	6,417
1965	Thelmal Lanes, Louisville	6,151
1966	Ace Mitchell Shur-Hooks, Akron	6,536
1967	Balancer Glove, Fort Worth	6,298
1968	Bowl-Rite Supply, Joliet, Illinois	6,285
1969	Dick Weber Wrist Masters, Santa Ana, California	6,413
1970*	Merchant Enterprises, New York	3,154
1971	Chester Iio Investments, Houston	3,081
1972	Basch Advertising, New York	3,099
1973	Stroh's Beer, Detroit	3,050
1974	Ebonite Corporation, Hopkinsville, Kentucky	3,117
1975	Munsingwear No. 2, Minneapolis	2,980
1976	Munsingwear No. 2, Minneapolis	3,281
1977	Columbia 300 Bowling Balls, San Antonio	3,122

*Format changed to six-team rolloff.

WIBC Open Team Champions

		Score
1969	Fitzpatrick Chevrolet, Concord, California	2,986
1970	Parker-Fothergill Pro Shop, Cranston, Rhode Island	3,034
1971	Koenig & Strey Real Estate, Wilmette, Illinois	2,891
1972	Angeltown Creations, Placentia, California	2,838
1973	Fitzpatrick Chevrolet, Concord, California	2,897
1974	Kalicak International Construction, St. Louis	2,973
1975	Atlanta Bowling Center (Ga. No. 1), Buffalo	2,836
1976	PWBA No. 1, Oklahoma City	2,839
1977	Allgauer's Restaurant, Chicago	2,818

ABC Classic Division All-Events Champions

		Score
1961	Bob Brayman	1,963
1962	Jack Winters	2,147
1963	Tom Hennessey	1,998
1964	Billy Hardwick	2,088
1965	Tom Hennessey	2,549
1966	Les Schissler	2,112
1967	Bob Strampe	2,092
1968	Jim Stefanich	1,983

WIBC Open All-Events Champions

		Score
1969	Helen Duval	1,927
1970	Dorothy Fothergill	1,984
1971	Lorrie Nichols	1,840
1972	Mildred Martorella	1,877
1973	Toni Calvery	1,910
1974	Judy Soutar	1,944
1975	Virginia (Park) Norton	1,821
1976	Betty Morris	1,866
1977	Akiko Yamaga	1,895

ABC Masters Champions

		W-L	Average
1951	Lee Jouglard	6-1	201.29
1952*	Willard Taylor	8-1	200.89
1953*	Rudy Habetler	10-1	200.30
1954	Eugene Elkins	7-0	205.68
1955	Buzz Fazio	7-0	204.46
1956	Dick Hoover	7-1	209.28
1957*	Dick Hoover	9-1	216.98
1958	Tom Hennessey	7-0	209.54
1959	Ray Bluth	7-0	214.93
1960	Billy Golembiewski	7-0	206.46
1961*	Don Carter	8-1	211.50
1962	Billy Golembiewski	7-0	223.43
1963	Harry Smith	7-0	219.12
1964	Billy Welu	7-0	227.00
1965*	Billy Welu	9-1	202.30
1966	Bob Strampe	7-0	219.29
1967	Lou Scalia	7-0	216.32
1968*	Pete Tountas	9-1	220.28
1969*	Jim Chestney	10-1	223.05
1970*	Don Glover	9-1	215.25
1971*	Jim Godman	9-1	229.20
1972*	Bill Beach	8-1	220.75
1973	Dave Soutar	7-0	218.61
1974	Paul Colwell	7-0	234.17
1975*	Ed Ressler, Jr.	9-1	213.57
1976	Nelson Burton, Jr.	7-0	220.79
1977	Earl Anthony	7-0	218.21

*From losers' bracket; won both matches in finals.

WIBC Queens Tournament Champions

	Winner	Runnerup
1961	Janet Harmon	Eula Touchette
1962	Dorothy Wilkinson	Marion Ladewig
1963*	Irene Monterossa	Georgette DeRosa
1964	D. D. Jacobson	Shirley Garms
1965	Betty Kuczynski	LaVerne Carter
1966*	Judy Lee	Nancy Peterson
1967	Millie Martorella	Phyllis Massey
1968*	Phyllis Massey	Marian Spencer
1969	Ann Feigel	Millie Martorella
1970	Millie Martorella	Joan Holm
1971*	Millie Martorella	Katherine Brown
1972	Dotty Fothergill	Maureen Harris
1973	Dotty Fothergill	Judy Soutar
1974	Judy Soutar	Betty Morris
1975*	Cindy Powell	Patty Costello
1976	Pam Rutherford	Shirley Sjostrom
1977	Dana Stewart	Vesma Grinfelds

*From losers' bracket; won both matches in finals.

All-Star/BPAA United States Open Champions

Men

	Winner	Winner's Average	Runnerup
1941	John Crimmins	206.93	Joe Norris
1942	Connie Schwoegler	213.36	Frank Benkovic
1943	Ned Day	208.92	Paul Krumske
1944	Buddy Bomar	205.80	Joe Wilman
1945	Joe Wilman	209.95	Therman Gibson
1946	Andy Varipapa	210.02	Allie Brandt
1947	Andy Varipapa	210.13	Joe Wilman
1948	Connie Schwoegler	211.84	Andy Varipapa
1949	Junie McMahon	210.38	Ralph Smith
1950	Dick Hoover	209.68	Lee Jouglard
1951	Junie McMahon	209.83	Bill Lillard
1952	Don Carter	204.75	Ed Lubanski
1954	Don Carter	207.06	Bill Lillard
1955	Steve Nagy	207.07	Ed Lubanski
1955	Bill Lillard	206.35	Joe Wilman
1956	Don Carter	208.12	Dick Weber
1958	Don Carter	213.72	Buzz Fazio
1959	Billy Welu	210.72	Ray Bluth
1960	Harry Smith	211.59	Bob Chase
1961	Bill Tucker	215.35	Dick Weber
1962	Dick Weber	214.16	Roy Lown
1963	Dick Weber	221.52	Billy Welu
1964	Bob Strampe	214.89	Tommy Tuttle
1965	Dick Weber	216.93	Jim St. John
1966	Dick Weber	219.26	Nelson Burton, Jr.
1967	Les Schissler	214.33	Pete Tountas
1968	Jim Stefanich	217.50	Billy Hardwick
1969	Billy Hardwick	219.54	Dick Weber
1970	Bobby Cooper	229.44	Billy Hardwick
1971	Mike Lemongello	215.52	Teata Semiz
1972	Don Johnson	215.42	George Pappas
1973	Mike McGrath	223.47	Earl Anthony
1974	Larry Laub	223.86	Dave Davis
1975	Steve Neff	222.92	Paul Colwell
1976	Paul Moser	212.25	Jim Frazier
1977	Johnny Petraglia	210.56	Bill Spigner

All-Star/BPAA United States Open Champions

Women

	Winner	Winner's Average	Runnerup
1949	Marion Ladewig	200.53	Catherine Burling
1950	Marion Ladewig	199.87	Stephanie Balogh
1951	Marion Ladewig	211.46	Sylvia Wene
1952	Marion Ladewig	204.34	Shirley Garms
1954	Marion Ladewig	196.87	Sylvia Wene
1955	Sylvia Wene	193.12	Sylvia Fanta
1955	Anita Cantaline	190.02	Doris Porter
1956	Marion Ladewig	194.11	Marge Merrick
1958	Merle Matthews	191.91	Marion Ladewig
1959	Marion Ladewig	201.03	Donna Zimmerman
1960	Sylvia Wene	193.95	Marion Ladewig
1961	Phyllis Notaro	194.46	Hope Ricilli
1962	Shirley Garms	199.02	Joy Abel
1963	Marion Ladewig	204.21	Bobbie Shaler
1964	LaVerne Carter	200.10	Evelyn Teal
1965	Ann Slattery	194.78	Sandy Hooper
1966	Joy Abel	198.95	Bette Rockwell
1967	Gloria Bouvia	195.52	Shirley Garms
1968	Dotty Fothergill	205.40	Doris Coburn
1969	Dotty Fothergill	203.67	Kayoka Suda
1970	Mary Baker	208.33	Judy Cook
1971	Paula Sperber	204.58	June Llewellyn
1972	Lorrie Koch	197.46	Mary Baker
1973	Millie Martorella	212.83	Patty Costello
1974	Patty Costello	196.67	Betty Morris
1975	Paula Sperber	199.48	Lorrie Koch
1976	Patty Costello	226.27	Betty Morris
1977	Betty Morris	207.10	Virginia Norton

BPAA TEAM MATCH RESULTS

Full Team Names and Represented Cities
(in alphabetical order)

Budweiser Beer, St. Louis
Clark Supply Company, Milwaukee
De Luxe Weld, Detroit
Don Carter Glove, St. Louis
E&B Beer, Detroit *(later changed to* **Pfeiffer Beer***)*
Edmonds Oldsmobile, Detroit
Falstaff Beer, St. Louis
Gold Bond Beer, Cleveland

Hamm's Beer, Chicago
Harper Tire Co., Chicago
Heil Products, Milwaukee
Helin Tackle, Detroit
Hermann Undertakers, St. Louis
Kathryn, Inc., Chicago *(later changed to* Tavern Pale*)*
Knudten Brothers Paints, Milwaukee
Lakepointe Chrysler, Detroit
Linsz Recreation, Cleveland
Lubanski Five, Detroit
Maibach Furniture, Akron
Meister Brau, Chicago *(later changed to* King Louie*)*
National Bowler's Journal, New York
Pabst Blue Ribbon, Chicago
Phillies Cigars, Philadelphia
Reserve Beer, Chicago
Rosatto-Barry, Philadelphia
Stroh's Beer, Detroit
Waldorf Lagers, Cleveland

	Winner	Loser	Margin in pins
Dec. 1934	Stroh	Hermann	330
Feb. 1935	Heil	Stroh	191
Mar. 1935	Heil	Rosatto-Barry	782
Apr. 1935	Heil	Waldorf	223
Jan. 1936	Heil	Pabst	1,177
Mar. 1937	Heil	Budweiser	1,148
Dec. 1938	Hermann	Heil	647
Dec. 1940	Hermann	Linsz	183
Feb. 1942	Bowlers Journal	Hermann	955
Nov. 1942	Stroh	Bowlers Journal	523
Mar. 1943	Stroh	Budweiser	462
Feb. 1944	Stroh	Rosatto-Barry	1,189
Dec. 1944	Stroh	Linsz	278
Apr. 1945	Stroh	Heil	696
Nov. 1945	E&B	Stroh	254
Jan. 1946	Meister Brau	E&B	104
Dec. 1946	Meister Brau	Clark Supply	137
Mar. 1947	Meister Brau	Phillies	1,219
Nov. 1947	Kathryn	Meister Brau	1,111
Mar. 1948	Kathryn	E&B	281
Nov. 1948	Tavern Pale	Knudten	805
Apr. 1949	Tavern Pale	De Luxe Weld	1,586
Nov. 1949	E&B	Tavern Pale	308
Mar. 1950	E&B	Gold Bond	1,167
Nov. 1950	E&B	Meister Brau	931
Mar. 1951	E&B	Stroh	365
Nov. 1951	E&B	Stroh	392
Mar. 1952	E&B	King Louie	275
Nov. 1952	Stroh	Pfeiffer	322
Dec. 1953	Stroh	Pfeiffer	167
Dec. 1954	Stroh	Maibach	1,355
Jan. 1956	Budweiser	Stroh	747
Jan. 1957	Budweiser	Falstaff	1,064
Nov. 1957	Falstaff	Reserve	860
1959	Budweiser	Falstaff	1.994 points
1960	Falstaff	Lubanski Five	0.835 points
1961	Don Carter Glove	Stroh	0.59 points
1962	Don Carter Glove	Helin	2.166 points
1963	Falstaff	Harper	4.041 points
1964	Lakepointe Chrysler	Stroh	204
1965	Hamm	Edmonds Olds	315

World's Invitational Champions

Men

1957	Don Carter
1958	Ed Lubanski
1959	Don Carter
1960	Don Carter
1961	Don Carter
1962	Don Carter
1963	Jim St. John
1964	Jim St. John

Women

1957	Marion Ladewig
1958	Charlotte Grubic
1959	Olga Gloor
1960	Marion Ladewig
1961	Marge Merrick
1962	Marion Ladewig
1963	Marion Ladewig
1964	Marion Ladewig

PBA Tournament of Champions Winners

		Average
1962	Joe Joseph	225.33
1963	No tournament	
1964	No tournament	
1965	Billy Hardwick	222.12
1966	Wayne Zahn	223.21
1967	Jim Stefanich	236.14
1968	Dave Davis	212.39
1969	Jim Godman	219.21
1970	Don Johnson	233.73
1971	Johnny Petraglia	215.40
1972	Mike Durbin	231.19
1973	Jim Godman	211.80
1974	Earl Anthony	212.76
1975	Dave Davis	221.04
1976	Marshall Holman	216.82
1977	Mike Berlin	216.22

246

Bowlers of the Year

Selected by the Bowling Writers Association of America

Men

1942	Johnny Crimmins
1943	Ned Day
1944	Ned Day
1945	Buddy Bomar
1946	Joe Wilman
1947	Buddy Bomar
1948	Andy Varipapa
1949	Connie Schwoegler
1950	Junie McMahon
1951	Lee Jouglard
1952	Steve Nagy
1953	Don Carter
1954	Don Carter
1955	Steve Nagy
1956	Bill Lillard
1957	Don Carter
1958	Don Carter
1959	Ed Lubanski
1960	Don Carter
1961	Dick Weber
1962	Don Carter
1963	Dick Weber
1964	Billy Hardwick
1965	Dick Weber
1966	Wayne Zahn
1967	Dave Davis
1968	Jim Stefanich
1969	Billy Hardwick
1970	Nelson Burton, Jr.
1971	Don Johnson
1972	Don Johnson
1973	Don McCune
1974	Earl Anthony
1975	Earl Anthony
1976	Earl Anthony
1977	Mark Roth

Bowlers of the Year

Selected by the Bowling Writers Association of America

Women

1948	Val Mikiel
1949	Val Mikiel
1950	Marion Ladewig
1951	Marion Ladewig
1952	Marion Ladewig
1953	Marion Ladewig
1954	Marion Ladewig
1955	Sylvia Wene
1956	Anita Cantaline
1957	Marion Ladewig
1958	Marion Ladewig
1959	Marion Ladewig
1960	Sylvia Wene
1961	Shirley Garms
1962	Shirley Garms
1963	Marion Ladewig
1964	LaVerne Carter
1965	Betty Kuczynski
1966	Joy Abel
1967	Millie Martorella
1968	Dotty Fothergill
1969	Dotty Fothergill
1970	Mary Baker
1971	Paula Sperber
1972	Patty Costello
1973	Judy Soutar
1974	Betty Morris
1975	Judy Soutar
1976	Patty Costello
1977	Betty Morris

Sparemaker

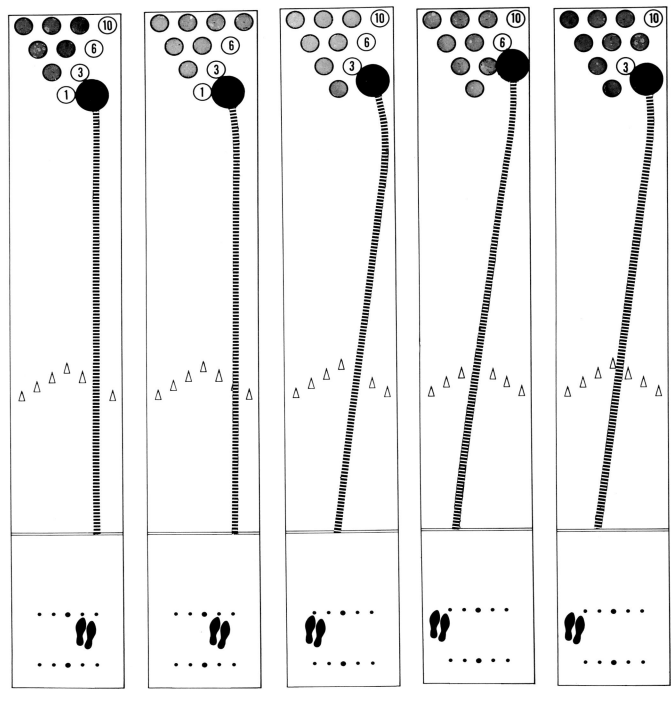

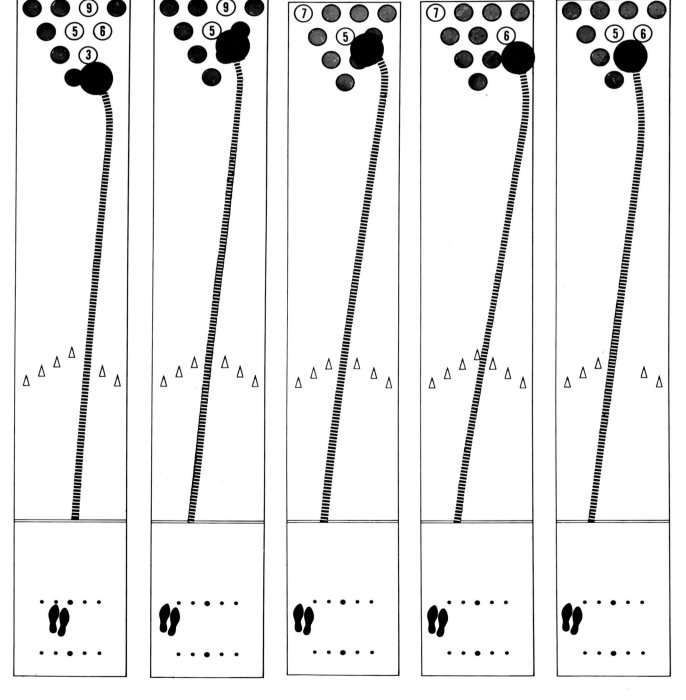

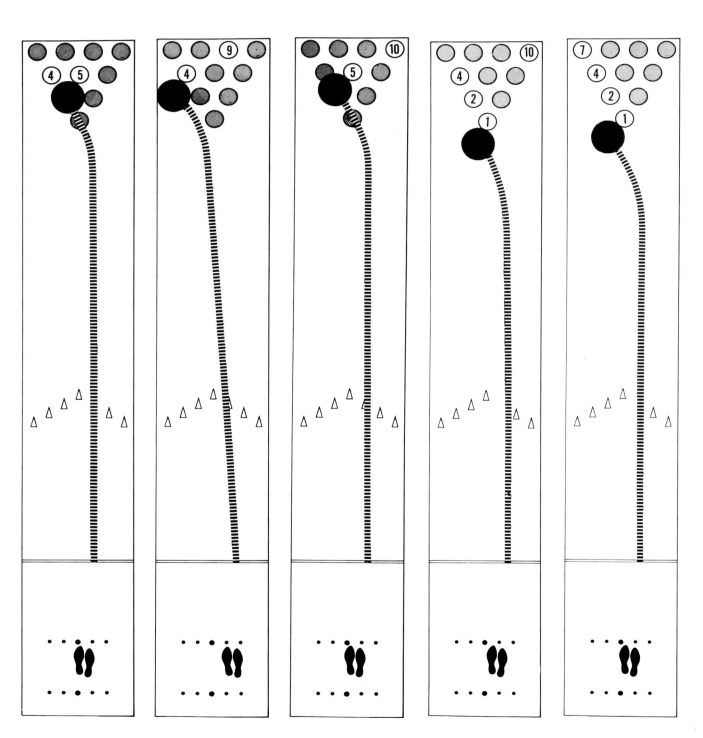

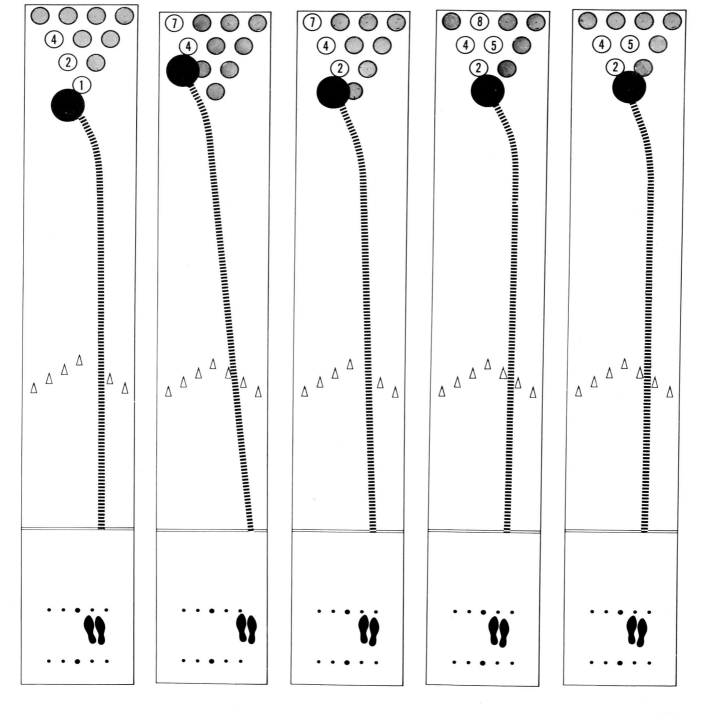

Ball Measurement

PITCH — The pitch of a hole is the angle at which the hole is drilled into the ball with relationship to the center of the ball. Four basic pitches are used in drilling a bowling ball: forward, reverse, right lateral and left lateral.

FORWARD PITCH — Center line of hole forward of center of ball.

REVERSE PITCH — Center line of hole away from center of ball.

RIGHT LATERAL PITCH — Under or toward the palm of the hand.

LEFT LATERAL PITCH — Away from palm of hand.

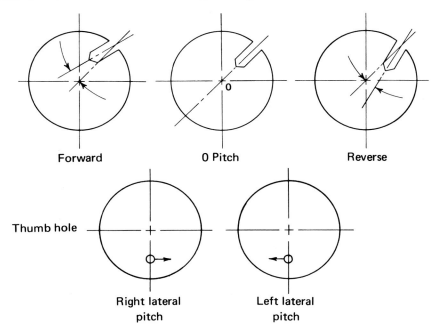

Note: Lateral pitches are often referred to as SIDE PITCHES. In right and left pitches, opposite is true for left-handed bowlers.

Another helpful way of relating forward, reverse, right and left pitches is to pinpoint the pitch in reference to the emblem of the bowling ball. Any drilling toward the emblem is forward pitch; a drilling away from the emblem is reverse pitch. Right and left lateral pitches are simply drillings toward the right or left of the emblem.

For many years pitches recommended almost universally, and widely used, were 3/8" forward pitch in the fingers and thumb with no side or lateral pitch. This was and still is known as the conventional grip.

Today there should be no such thing as a conventional grip! Conventional type grip, yes; strict conventional, no. Every customer should have his own custom drilled ball without any preconceived notions as to what the drilling should be. Every hand is as different as every fingerprint, and adjustments, no matter how small, should be made.

CONVENTIONAL GRIP—

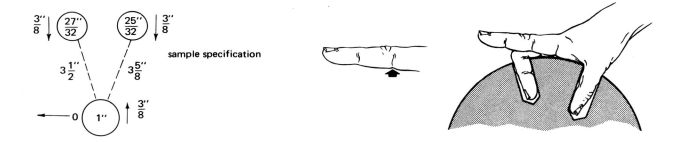

sample specification

STRETCH FINGERTIP GRIP—

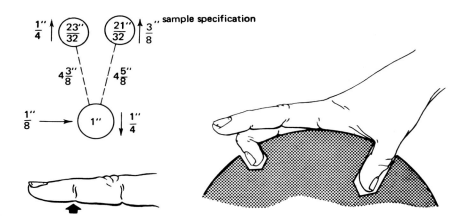

sample specification

A *semi-fingertip* is the compromise between the conventional and fingertip grip as it is measured somewhere between the second crease used for a conventional and the first crease for the full fingertip.

Theoretically, the semi-fingertip should then give the advantages of the conventional and fingertip. In practice it usually does not work out that way. Since the semi is drilled between the creases, it is doubtful that the bowler will insert his fingers the same way each time. This, in turn, makes it difficult for the ball measurer and driller to come up with pitches which will make the ball feel the same all the time.

In most cases, then, it is more desirable to go to the conventional or the fingertip. A "wide" conventional or a "relaxed" fingertip can achieve the same aims of the semi-fingertip — with none of the disadvantages.

The *fingertip ball* provides more leverage for the bowler, resulting in a ball with more revolutions. A fingertip is also easier on the hand. Pros and other bowlers who roll many games find the fingertip causes them less physical wear and tear than any other type of drilling.

Index

Acknowledgments

Many people generously contributed their knowledge, suggestions, and support to this book. Aside from all the information and assistance they provided, they made it clear just in the way they helped that the bowling community is the friendliest in all of sports. The author and editors wish to thank:

Dave De Lorenzo, Steve James, Sharon Vitrano, Jeanne Hofmann and Andy Stuart of the American Bowling Congress (ABC); Bill Bunetta, Jack Graziano, Andrew Hamel, Henry Kavan, Marianne Koestner, Victoria Marin, Mike Matera, Tom Meade, Sam Morales, Al Spanjer, Dick Weber, and Woody Woodruff of AMF Bowling Products Group in New York; Leo Eldridge, Mark Plotnick, Rosemary Oblinger, Bud Clabaugh, Mitch Clay, Fred Gross, and Bob Hartge of AMF Bowling Products Group in Shelby, Ohio; Jim Dressel and Mort Luby Jr. of *Bowlers Journal*; Vladimir ("Chief") Wapensky and Bert Zitek of the Bowling Proprietors' Association of America; Milt Rudo and Arthur Serbo of the Brunswick Corporation; Joe Kissel of the *Chicago Bowler*; John Jowdy of Columbia Industries Incorporated; Remo Picchietti and Doc Kuchen of DBA Industries, Inc.; the management of Melville Bowl, Melville, New York; Keith Satter and Russ Wapensky of the National Bowling Council (NBC); Ed Marcou and Bruce Pluckhahn of the National Bowling Hall of Fame and Museum; Joe Antenora, Pete Englehart, Bud Fisher, Harry Golden, Jerry Levine, and Larry Lichstein of the Professional Bowlers Association (PBA); Pat McDonough of the *Sports Reporter*; Carl Nicolay of the United Bowling Clubs; John Andresen of the Williamsburg Bowling Club; Alberta Crowe, Augie Karcher, and Helen Latham of the Women's International Bowling Congress (WIBC); Roger Blaemire, Janet Buehler, Toni Murray and Wyatt Slaughter of the Women's Professional Bowlers Association; and, independently, Buddy Bomar, Steve Cruchon, Mark Collor, Avin Mark Domnitz, Hy Domnitz, Eddie Elias, Leo M. Grawey, Eddie Krems, Paul Krumske, John Lawrence, Chuck Pezzano, Myrtle Schulte, Violet ("Billy") Simon, Billy Sixty, Don Snyder and Lucille Ware.

Special thanks to the ABC, AMF Bowling Products Group, *Bowlers Journal*, DBA, Inc., the National Bowling Hall of Fame and Museum, the PBA, and the WIBC all for the use of their pictures and for their extraordinary cooperation in the photo researching of this book.

Finally, we are indebted to AMF Bowling Products Group for helping to promote this project and to AMF's Al Spanjer and Jack Graziano for coordinating it.

Photo Credits

American Bowling Congress (ABC)
10–11, 12 top, 14 bottom, 16 right, 18–19, 20–21, 23, 24 all, 25, 42 bottom, 44, 46–47, 48, 49, 52, 59, 60 right, 62, 63 all, 65 left, 67 top, 68 all, 69 all, 71 top and middle, 73, 74, 77 all, 81 bottom left, 82, 83 all, 85, 86 all, 87, 88–89, 90 top, 91, 93, 95 left, 135, 156–7, 172 all, 173 all, 218, 228, 228–29, 232 all, 233 all, 234, 235 right, 237 bottom left, 239 all

ABC testing facility
160–61, 161 all, 177 all, 178, 179 all, 181 bottom

AMF Bowling Products Group
8, 12 top, 15, 38–39, 39 right, 45, 65 right, 67 bottom, 75 all, 90 bottom, 143 bottom, 150 right, 166 all, 168 all, 169 all, 189 right top and bottom, 190 all, 198, 211, 224

Bowlers Journal
13 top and bottom right, 84 middle, 97 top, 132, 134, 143 top, 144, 145, 151 left, 152 all, 158, 167 all, 236

Bowling Hall of Fame
14 top, 22 top, 39 left, 41, 42 top, 46 bottom, 50 all, 51, 57, 60 left, 76, 79 top, 81 top, bottom right, 84 right, 95 right, 151 right, 164 all, 165 all, 215 all, 219, 220, 230–31, 235 left, 237 top left and right, bottom right

Brown Brothers   46 top, 53

Janet Buehler   142 bottom

Chicago Bowler   61, 79 bottom, 84 left

Claster Television Productions   99

Melchior DiGiacomo   112–13

DBA, Inc.   174 all, 175 all, 180 all, 181 top

Kendall Lanes   98 all

Peter Read Miller
6–7, 101, 104, 108, 109 all, 113, 116, 117 all, 120, 182–83, 184, 185 all, 186 all, 187 all, 188 all, 189 left top and bottom, 191 all, 192 all, 193 all, 194, 195 all, 196 all, 197 all, 199 all

Jack and Peter Mecca
103 all, 106, 107, 106–07, 110, 111 all, 114, 115, 118 all, 119, 123 all, 124–25, 125 all, 127 all, 129 all, 138 all

Museum of the City of New York   36

New York Public Library
22 middle and bottom, 28 all, 32, 33

Al Panzera
147, 148, 148–49, 150 left, 154, 155 all

Bruce Pluckhahn
1, 2–3, 26–27, 30–31 all, 34, 35 all, 56 all

Professional Bowlers Association (PBA)
96, 97 bottom, 130 all, 137, 211, 227, 238 all

Lucille Ware   223

Allan Weitz   201–02, 204, 205, 206, 206–07, 208, 209

Women's International Bowling Congress (WIBC)
13 left, 16 left, 17, 43, 54 all, 55, 70, 71 bottom, 133, 140–41, 153

Women's Professional Bowlers Association (WPBA)   142 top